Metro Dailies in the Age of Multimedia Journalism

Metro Dailies in the Age of Multimedia Journalism

MARY LOU NEMANIC

TEMPLE UNIVERSITY PRESS
Philadelphia • Rome • Tokyo

TEMPLE UNIVERSITY PRESS
Philadelphia, Pennsylvania 19122
tupress.temple.edu

Published 2020

Library of Congress Cataloging-in-Publication Data

Names: Nemanic, Mary Lou, 1950– author.
Title: Metro dailies in the age of multimedia journalism / Mary Lou Nemanic.
Description: Philadelphia : Temple University Press, [2020] | Includes bibliographical references and index. | Summary: "Examines U.S. metro dailies, the newspapers hit hardest by declines in advertising and circulation, and how they continue to survive and contribute important news coverage despite predictions that they would eventually wither away."— Provided by publisher.
Identifiers: LCCN 2019023580 (print) | LCCN 2019023581 (ebook) | ISBN 9781439916766 (cloth : alk. paper) | ISBN 9781439916773 (paperback : alk. paper) | ISBN 9781439916780 (pdf)
Subjects: LCSH: Newspaper publishing—Effect of technological innovations on—United States—Case studies. | American newspapers—Circulation—Case studies. | Journalists—Effect of technological innovations on—United States—Case studies. | Journalism, Regional—United States—History—21st century. Online journalism—United States—History—21st century.
Classification: LCC PN4888.C56 N38 2020 (print) | LCC PN4888.C56 (ebook) | DDC 071.3—dc23
LC record available at https://lccn.loc.gov/2019023580
LC ebook record available at https://lccn.loc.gov/2019023581

♾ The paper used in this publication meets the requirements of the American National Standard for Information Sciences—Permanence of Paper for Printed Library Materials, ANSI Z39.48-1992

Printed in the United States of America

9 8 7 6 5 4 3 2 1

For the dedicated and passionate journalists who established the free press and for those who continue to protect it

Contents

Acknowledgments

I owe a great deal of thanks to the numerous people who helped me with my research and revisions. I am very grateful to all the journalists and former journalists who took time out of their incredibly busy schedules to be interviewed. These include Tyler Batiste, Tom Birdsong, Jen Bjorhus, Gus Chan, Samantha Christmann, Brian Connolly, David Denney, Lisa DeYoung, Rachel Dissell, Mark Dolan, Chris Evans, Thom Fladung, Ben Garvin, Jim Gehrz, Colleen Kelley, David Kordalski, Patrick LaKamp, Neal Lambert, Michelle LaVigne, Rich Lee, Tim McDonough, Wendy McManamon, Sara Meehan, Kevin O'Brien, Dave Orrick, Tim O'Shei, Deb Pastner, Brian Peterson, Holly Peterson, Jenni Pinkley, Julia Rendleman, George Rodrigue, Mila Sanina, David Sherman, David Shribman, Jonathan Silver, Charlie Specht, Stephanie Strasburg, Margaret Sullivan, Tom Sweeney, Sandy Tan, Lillian Thomas, Ben Tsujimoto, Kurt Weber, MaryJo Webster, Jen Westpfahl, Paul Wieland, and the professionals who requested to be interviewed anonymously. I also thank the staff of Temple University Press, especially editor Aaron Javsicas, Joan S. Vidal, Gary Kramer, and Ashley Petrucci; copyeditor Virginia Perrin; and the anonymous manuscript reviewers for Temple University Press, who provided important recommendations for revisions.

In addition, I am grateful to the faculty, administration, and staff of the Pennsylvania State University–Altoona for their help and support: Bob Trumpbour, Brian Black, Nick Mohammed, Lori Bechtel-Wherry, Jeff Knapp, Cindy McCarty, Gale Biddle, Jen Phillips, Tracy Reilly, and Kay Tate. Finally, I thank my husband, Doug Nemanic, a veteran journalist whose insights and support have been most appreciated.

Metro Dailies in the Age of Multimedia Journalism

Introduction

The Crises Facing Newspapers

> Newspapers have been frequently portrayed as dinosaurs on the verge of extinction. . . . [M]any people assume they will be unable to compete with new forms of electronic media and therefore will eventually die out. That assumption, however, underestimates the adaptability of newspapers and their importance in both contemporary and future societies. (Fidler 1997, 251)

Media scholar Roger Fidler's assessment of the future of newspapers, in his seminal book, *Mediamorphosis* (1997), is still true more than twenty years later. Despite competition from the Internet and steep recessionary declines in revenue, U.S. newspapers have survived and are slowly adapting to new technologies and multiplatform content delivery. In the second decade of the twenty-first century, they still provide the majority of the country's original reporting compared to online news sources (Barthel 2016; Brüggemann et al. 2016; Schizer 2011; Associated Press 2010; Pew 2010; Fritz 2010).

Nonetheless, newspapers are struggling as they face both a financial crisis due to decades of annually declining advertising revenue and decreasing circulation numbers and an identity crisis as they continue to slowly transition from print-only to multiplatform and multimedia content delivery. Significantly, within the newspaper industry, metro dailies, with their high operating costs, have been hit hardest (Barthel 2015a, 2015b, 2016; Doctor 2015a). At the heart of the newspaper crisis is a flawed business model that relies on advertising rather than subscriptions or other forms of revenue (Barthel 2015b, 2016; Brady 2016; Doctor 2015a; Phillips 2014; Ryfe 2012). Because of the annual decreases in advertising revenue, especially the steep declines precipitated by the recession of 2007, many newspapers have been attempting to decrease their dependence on advertising and obtain more of their revenue from subscriptions and from non-news sources (Pew 2018).

The identity crisis facing newspapers involves adapting from text-based newsroom practices to multimedia practices that include video, audio, and still photography. These responsibilities are often expected of news staffs without the adequate training necessary for proficiency in visual journalism or increased salaries to compensate for greater workloads (Brüggemann et al. 2016; Ekdale et al. 2015; Phillips 2014; Lee-Wright, Phillips, and Witschge 2011; Witschge and Nygren 2009). Significantly, this identity crisis is evident in a clash between traditional print journalism's formality and emphasis on detail and digital journalism's informality and brevity. The values and practices of print and online journalism also reflect this disparity. Traditional print journalism emphasizes a full vetting of sources before publishing a story, journalistic detachment, professional photojournalistic storytelling, and reporters as the authoritative voices of their newspapers. In contrast, digital journalism typically challenges these practices by emphasizing breaking news, using iterative reporting (or reporting in short posts as a story is developing), encouraging the personal involvement of journalists with their audiences, and inviting readers to contribute comments, stories, and photographs (Phillips 2014; Lee-Wright, Phillips, and Witschge 2011; Witschge and Nygren 2009).

Traditionally, print journalism has emphasized journalistic autonomy from government and commercial influences and the maintenance of separate roles for reporters and photojournalists under the protection of newspaper guilds as well as autonomy in news practices that includes resistance to corporate quotas for daily story and multimedia postings. In contrast, digital journalism reflects a different perspective on journalistic autonomy, often equating it with spatial independence from the newsroom, and some Digital-First operations hire nonunion backpack journalists who are required to not only report from the field but also produce photos and videos (Phillips 2014; Shister 2010). Reporters in these positions often face quotas for daily online postings.

Overall, despite the fact that newspapers have survived and many are still marginally profitable, the debate persists about whether or not the crises are so severe that newspapers are dying. This debate has intensified since the recession of 2007, which substantially accelerated annual declines in advertising and circulation. The losses also forced many newspapers to close or eliminate their print editions and become digital-only publications (Edge 2014a; Waldman 2011). One of the most widely publicized narratives about the death of newspapers was issued in 2011 by the University of Southern California's Annenberg Center for the Digital Future, which predicted that most print newspapers would be gone by 2016, leaving only four major daily newspapers: the *New York Times, USA Today,* the *Washington Post,* and the *Wall Street Journal* (Romero 2011; Sonderman 2011). Although in 2019 this prediction was far from materializing, newspapers are in crisis nonetheless (Brüggemann et al. 2016; Barthel 2016; Doctor 2016a; Edmonds 2016c; Chyi 2013; Edge 2014a, 2014b).

Former *USA Today* columnist and former editor of the *American Journalism Review* Rem Rieder agreed with the assessment that newspapers are not necessarily on the verge of extinction and that many are still profitable.

> They are still here. Battered, beleaguered, but still here. Which is hardly to say that they aren't endangered. The advent of the digital age has thoroughly disrupted the

> industry, dramatically shrinking ad revenue and making the days of eye-popping profits a distant memory. The newspaper business is in a desperate struggle to reinvent itself for the digital world. (2016a)

While the industry's financial crisis has typically been attributed to technological change (the Internet and digitization) and the recession of 2007–2009, some argue that newspaper management missteps should not be neglected. Stephen Lacy, Michael Stamm, and Hugh Martin contend that cost-containment policies are major factors that are often overlooked in accounts of the crisis. Their research showed that "managerial short-run decisions from 1985–2005 contributed greatly to the current crisis" (Lacy, Stamm, and Martin 2014, 6). These decisions included "creating clusters of commonly owned newspapers, eliminating high-cost circulation at the edges of local markets and cutting newsroom costs by reducing newsroom staffs. All of these measures resulted in declining circulation and market penetration" (Lacy, Stamm, and Martin 2014, 7).

Generally, staff reductions have been implemented through layoffs, buyouts, and attrition. In fact, according to a 2016 Pew Research report, in the past twenty years, "the newspaper workforce has shrunk by about 20,000 positions, or 39%" (Barthel 2016). In 2018, Pew reported that between 2007 and 2017 newspaper newsrooms had shrunk by almost half, or 45 percent (Grieco 2018). Some particularly drastic cuts included the *New Orleans Times-Picayune,* which in 2012 lost nearly one-third its newsroom staff, and the *Cleveland Plain Dealer,* which in 2013 lost nearly one-third of its news staff, as detailed in Chapter 3 of this volume (Edge 2014a, 2014b; Clark 2013; White 2012). Lacy and his colleagues noted that several studies indicated the connection between divestment in print operations and declines in circulation (Lacy, Stamm, and Martin 2014). Nonetheless, despite criticism from analysts and scholars on the pressure of newsroom reductions on surviving staffs, many managers continue to rationalize the cutbacks by contending their staffs can "do more with less" and still deliver quality content in print and 24/7 online (Reinardy 2016; Rieder 2014).

Refuting this contention is Scott Reinardy's powerful ethnographic study, *Journalism's Lost Generation,* which presents an inside perspective on how increased workloads and the accelerated pace of the 24/7 news cycle have affected news staffs. Reinardy's research clearly documents the destruction of newsroom morale and the widespread burnout of newspapers' "most valuable resources"—their staffs (2016, 101).

Similarly, *Tales from the Great Disruption: Insights and Lessons from Journalism's Technological Transformation,* by Michael Shapiro, Anna Hiatt, and Mike Hoyt, details the diminished aspects of newspapers (Shapiro, Hiatt, and Hoyt 2015). They contend that short-term efforts such as periodic layoffs are obstacles to producing quality content and incorporating innovation into news practices and that this basically amounts to "eating your seed corn" (Shapiro, Hiatt, and Hoyt 2015, 199).

The Digital-First Debate

Media scholars Iris Chyi and Ori Tenenboim have also criticized many newspaper owners and executives for adopting the "Digital-First" (or reverse publication) approach that prioritizes and invests in online platforms at the expense of print (Chyi and Tenenboim 2017; Doctor 2015b). In this essay and in Chyi's 2013 book, *Trial and Error,* owners and managers are criticized for ignoring scholarly research and relying on the advice of consultants such as Harvard professor Clayton Christensen. Christensen's disruptive innovation theory is the basis for the Digital-First approach, which asserts that new technologies will open up new markets that will disrupt and eventually displace older markets (Christensen 1997). In the case of newspapers, print is assumed to be dying, and the future is assumed to be all digital. In light of this theory, Christensen advised newspaper corporations to de-emphasize their print operations, invest in online operations, separate online from print operations, and be willing to tolerate lower online profit margins in the short term until the new online markets have developed (Christensen 1997; Edmonds 2014b).

Debunking the Digital-First approach, Chyi and Tenenboim argue that the results of twenty years of online experiments have been "underwhelming" (Chyi and Tenenboim 2017, 2). In their quantitative study of more than fifty metro dailies between the years 2007 and 2015, they concluded that print continues to be the "core product" in local markets, with online readership showing "little or no growth during that period" (14). In addition, they found print "surpassed online reach by a wide margin across all age groups" (11). On average, the websites they studied attained only about a 10 percent market penetration. Their research was reinforced in 2018 by an American Press Institute finding that 71 percent of newspaper subscribers "prefer or only use the print paper, 26% prefer or only use digital content, and 3% do not have a preference" (Media Insight Project, 2018).

In 2017, the publication of Chyi and Tenenboim's study sparked an online debate between scholars and media analysts defending the Digital-First strategy and those who envision print as a viable platform within an array of platforms for delivering news content (Buttry 2016; Brown-Smith and Groves 2016; Shafer 2016). The most caustic attack came from scholar and newspaper veteran Steve Buttry, who calls their findings "B.S." and criticizes them for overemphasizing the prevalence of the Digital-First strategy. He argues:

> Well, I used to work for a company called Digital First Media and at a newspaper-industry think tank, and I've visited more than 100 newsrooms and spoken at more than 100 newspaper-industry conferences and seminars, and I can flatly say that the industry never, ever adopted anything close to a digital-first strategy. . . . When I worked at Digital First, I described our company's name as an aspiration, rather than an achievement. (Buttry 2016)

While acknowledging that newspapers have been doing "a lousy job of generating digital revenue," Buttry argues that this was only because they did not use more aggressive online strategies (2016; Brown-Smith and Groves 2016). But Chyi and Tenenboim, as well as media scholar Marc Edge, maintain that online advertising is not very lucrative for newspaper sites not only because the Internet is so competitive in terms of news outlets but also because studies show that the aggregators and social media sites, not newspaper sites, gain the largest share of online advertising profits (Chyi and Tenenboim 2017; Edge 2014a, 2014b; Chyi 2013).

While the debate continues over Digital First Media's strategies, there can be no doubt that "Digital First" characterizes those strategies implemented by Advance Publications, particularly at the *New Orleans Times-Picayune* and at the *Cleveland Plain Dealer* (detailed in Chapter 3 of this volume). Despite protests from readers and advertisers in both cities and harsh criticism from industry analysts, in 2012 and 2013 Advance reduced publication days and home-delivery days in New Orleans and home-delivery days in Cleveland. At both papers, Advance separated the print and online operations and drastically reduced the print staffs (McQuaid 2012; Edge 2014a; Theim 2013a, 2013b, 2015; Clark 2013; Sterne 2013; Edmonds 2014a). The company's Digital-First policies were also criticized for their emphasis on rapid and frequent postings of stories-in-progress at the expense of accuracy and balance and for their preoccupation with posting stories that generate clicks rather than stories based on quality journalism and public service (Beaujon et al. 2014; Clark 2014b, 2014c; see also Chapter 3 herein).

Newspapers Are Still Viable

The in-depth interviews conducted for this book and my examination of the scholarly and industry research have convinced me that there is a future for newspapers as they continue to transition into multiplatform content delivery. Metro dailies, in particular, can continue to survive if companies are willing to integrate their print and online operations, are committed to visual journalism, and retain staff sizes substantial enough to allow for quality content. It should be noted that visual journalism is an essential piece of this argument, given the powerful attraction of images in print and digital layouts (S. Quinn 2015; Walker 2012; Bucher and Schumacher 2006). Significantly, as detailed in this book's case studies, newspapers have the best chance for success when owners allow journalists to manage their newspapers to ensure production of quality journalism under the protection of newspaper guilds. This is evident at the *Minneapolis Star Tribune,* where the owner, a civic benefactor, refrains from interfering in its daily operations.

Unfortunately, the current trend of hedge fund and corporate ownership preoccupied with quarterly profits has been particularly devastating to newspapers, as detailed in Chapters 3 and 5. These chapters focus on the layoffs and resource cutbacks that have jeopardized quality standards at the *Cleveland Plain Dealer* and the diminished staff and coverage area of the *St. Paul Pioneer Press.* As media scholar Angela Phillips argues, journalistic autonomy, or "freedom from direct commercial or political constraints," can be ensured only with "some degree of editorial independence from the influence of companies that own them" (2014, 79). This autonomy has been safeguarded by newspaper guild representation, which is also under siege as some corporate owners use the industry's crisis as an opportunity to disable or eliminate unions, also discussed in Chapters 3 and 5.

The purpose of this book is to detail how five metro dailies and their staffs are adapting to the transition from print-only to multiplatform content delivery and how newsroom practices are evolving to address this change. Central themes throughout this book include what is lost when fewer journalists are expected to do more with less time and fewer resources and how metro dailies are experimenting with measures to generate profits and attract readers.

Overall, a key argument in *Metro Dailies* is that newspapers are still important within the contemporary multimedia landscape not only because they generate most of the revenue compared to their websites and readers prefer print to online platforms but also because newspapers provide more original reporting than online news operations and original reporting is crucial in a democracy for keeping the electorate informed (Mitchell and Holcomb 2016; Phillips 2014; Schizer 2011; Fritz 2010; Cardin 2009).

Significantly, *Metro Dailies* argues for an integrated multiplatform approach to content delivery in which print and online platforms are considered complementary and in which visual journalism is emphasized across platforms. This argument rejects both the Digital-First and the printcentric approaches to content delivery, instead advocating for an approach that journalists at the *St. Paul Pioneer Press* call "Digital Right." This approach involves debuting content on the platform most appropriate to the complexity of the story and having the ability to reach the largest number of readers via the platform on a particular day (e.g., Sunday versus a weekday) or at a particular time of day. In addition, to deal with the difficulty of integrating the practices of print and digital journalism, this book recommends adopting a hybrid approach to content delivery similar to that of the *Minneapolis Star Tribune.* This newspaper established a Quick Strike Team, a unit dedicated to fast-breaking news that updates the website frequently with brief stories in the iterative style that keeps readers up-to-date with breaking news. Other multimedia reporting teams and beat reporters concentrate on detailed and more analytical content across platforms that preserves print journalism's values of verification, balance, and in-depth coverage.

The integrated multiplatform approach advocated in this book is illuminated in the following brief case studies of metro dailies: the *Rocky Mountain News,* which neglected its digital operations, and the *New Orleans Times-Picayune,* which was converted to a Digital-First operation.

The Untimely Demise of the *Rocky Mountain News*

On February 27, 2009, the *Rocky Mountain News,* Colorado's oldest newspaper, published its last issue, leaving the *Denver Post* as the city's only metro daily. The recipient of four Pulitzer Prizes, the *Rocky Mountain News* built its reputation on stories on crime and corruption in Denver. During most of its lifespan, the newspaper competed intensely with the *Denver Post* for the metro audience, but by 2001 it was considered a failing newspaper, prompting analysts to declare that Denver, like so many other metro areas across the country, could no longer sustain two dailies (Frank 2009; Dealbook 2009).

Although the E. W. Scripps Company's ownership was "on a relatively healthy financial footing," the newspaper's losses in 2008 climbed to $16 million; consequently, it was put up for sale (Adams, Ovide, and Simon 2009). Despite the fact that the *Rocky Mountain News* "still managed a profit margin close to the industry average for the year: 10 percent," it was unable to find a buyer and was closed in 2009, leaving more than two hundred staff members without jobs (Frank 2009; Perez-Pena 2009; Kurtz 2009). Although its average weekday circulation of 210,281 was close to the *Denver Post*'s 210,585, the recession had triggered a steep drop in advertising revenue, while circulation had fallen by more than 50 percent, down from 446,000 in 2001. Rich Boehne, Scripps's chief executive, called the *Rocky Mountain News* "a victim of changing times in our industry and huge economic challenges" (Dealbook 2009).

But some found this uncomplicated rationale unconvincing because it neglected management's role in the paper's demise. Sportswriter Dave Krieger's perspective, written for the newspaper's last edition, was quoted in a *Time* article:

> I still don't get how a newspaper with 200,000 paying subscribers and hundreds of thousands more readers on the Web cannot make a go of it. . . . "Not our fault," the suits say. "[It's the] business model's fault." So who came up with the business model? (Diddlebock 2009)

While the recession and the Internet were certainly factors leading to the demise of the *Rocky Mountain News*, a column by *Time* writer Bob Diddlebock also blamed "Scripps's newspaper executives[,] whose ineptitude over the past 25 years fumbled away a prime market to a competitor they should have killed off two decades ago" (2009).

Reinforcing this position, former publisher, president, and editor of the *Rocky Mountain News* John Temple tied the paper's demise to several management missteps that failed to integrate its print and online operations. These included initially separating print and online operations, the neglect of strategies to engage online readers, and the general perception that the website was merely a supplement to the print platform (Temple 2009).

> You can see from this introduction to our first electronic service that we thought of ourselves as newspaper companies right from the start. We wrote that the goal of the new edition was "ultimately to strengthen and preserve the printed daily newspaper." (Temple 2009)

To succeed in today's media environment, Temple advised newspaper management to take advantage of digital technology opportunities, to experiment with different profit-generating strategies, and to build "many niches and many audiences." He explained that "newspaper companies have to look for ways to answer the needs of the people in their communities," yet they must stop thinking about a monolithic audience limited to a specific geographic market (Temple 2009).

The *New Orleans Times-Picayune* and the Shift to Digital First

The *New Orleans Times-Picayune* began publishing in 1837 under the name the *Picayune*. The name refers to a Spanish coin that was initially the price set for this newspaper. It became the *Times-Picayune* in 1914 after merging with its competitor, the *New Orleans Times-Democrat*. In 1962 it was purchased by the Newhouse Family, owners of the New York–based Advance Publications (McQuaid 2012; Edge 2014a; Theim 2013b, 2015).

The *Times-Picayune* is well known for its community coverage, most notably in 2005 in the wake of Hurricane Katrina, when many staff members chose to remain in the newsroom to publish the newspaper and post news and community listings on the paper's website instead of evacuating to safety. The community listings included forums and blogs to provide citizens with resources and to assist first responders. This work was acknowledged by a Pulitzer Prize for Public Service as well as individual Pulitzer Prizes for four of the paper's staff members (Farhi 2015; Theim 2013b; Yu 2014).

In 2012 the *Times-Picayune*'s parent company, Advance Publications, established a Digital-First strategy to reduce print publications to three days a week. Because more than one-third of New Orleans residents did not have high-speed Internet and "the seven-day-a-week reading habit" was engrained in readers whose paper had one of the highest metro daily penetration rates in the United States, Advance's strategy caused an uproar (Farhi 2015; Hamm 2013a). Rebecca Theim, a former *Times-Picayune* reporter, described the reaction of readers and businesses to Advance's plans:

> Almost immediately, the community went berserk. A grassroots campaign included dedicated Facebook pages and Twitter accounts with thousands of followers, an online petition that eventually garnered close to 10,000 signatures, 1,500 yard signs supporting a daily newspaper, and public protests. (2015)

In addition, a number of national celebrities such as professional athlete Archie Manning and jazz musician Winton Marsalis, representing the *Times-Picayune* Citizens Group, sent an open letter to the New York–based Newhouse family requesting they sell the newspaper to local owners (Edge 2014a; Theim 2013b). However, Advance refused to sell and went ahead with its Digital-First initiative, which resulted in laying off nearly one-third of the newsroom. Advance also restructured the newsroom, creating separate staffs and separate newsrooms for print and for the website, nola.com (Doctor 2013a). Despite their separation, the Digital-First policy required both staffs to contribute first to the website, after which the print staff would repurpose online content for the paper (Doctor 2012). Theim noted one staff member's description of the change: "We've gone from being a newspaper that posted some of our content online to being an online operation whose material is put into print" (Theim 2015).

Although for a short time in 2012 New Orleans was the largest U.S. city without a daily newspaper, the *Times-Picayune* returned to a seven-day-a-week publication schedule shortly after *The Advocate,* a Baton Rouge newspaper, launched its daily New Orleans edition (Farhi 2015; *New Orleans* Magazine 2016; Chittum 2013b; Yu 2014). Despite the *Times-Picayune*'s resuming a daily publication schedule, it reduced home deliveries to three days a week, with papers published on nondelivery days available only at newsstands (Myers 2012). Over time, *The Advocate* increased its circulation, until in 2015 it surpassed that of the *Times-Picayune,* making it Louisiana's largest newspaper (Griggs 2015).

Because Advance's Digital-First strategy focused on cost reduction rather than meeting the needs of the city's residents for print, an upstart daily was able to fulfill reader preferences and build a readership at the *Times-Picayune*'s expense. An article in the *Washington Post* quoted a reader who blamed Advance for the loss of so many *Times-Picayune* subscribers: "They chose to decimate their publication. . . . News is important to a community especially this one. And they made the decision not to be a viable newspaper." In the same article, a seventy-five-year old civic activist and philanthropist described the loss to the community: "The Times-Picayune set the tone of civic discussion [about] politics, about rebuilding, the educational system, you name it. You need that common voice. A web site isn't the same thing." In addition, Ricky Mathews, the president of the website, was asked whether or not Advance's Digital-First approach had been a success in New Orleans. To this he replied: "I don't think you can say that. . . . There's not a finish line that any of us see in the near future" (Farhi 2015).

Literature and Theoretical Foundations for *Metro Dailies*

Overall, the closing of the *Rocky Mountain News* after 150 years and the Digital-First conversion of the *New Orleans Times-Picayune* underscore the need for integrated multiplatform approaches for metro dailies and foreground the complicated challenges that persist as the newspaper industry faces crises both financially and existentially. Both newspapers highlight policy problems that result when owners or managers see profit as the mission of newspapers instead of serving communities and acting as watchdogs over government.

My argument that newspapers should adopt an integrated multiplatform approach with an emphasis on visual journalism stems from my interpretation of convergent media theory. As articulated by Henry Jenkins in his seminal book, *Convergence Culture,* this theory describes an ongoing process that is characterized by "the flow of content across multiple platforms" in which previously distinct media forms and platforms interact and complement each other (2006, 3).

In terms of the relationship between traditional media and new media platforms, Jenkins explains that "old media are not being displaced. Rather, their functions and status are shifted by the introduction of new technologies" and "the migratory behavior of media audiences" that use different media platforms for different needs and interests (2006, 14, 2). This contrasts with Christensen's technologically deterministic theory of disruptive innovation in which new media displace traditional media platforms (1997). Instead, by taking a social constructivist approach, Jenkins details the actual *process* of adapting to new technologies and the social, cultural, and economic factors relating to this process (2006). Consequently, Jenkins's convergence theory challenges extreme approaches such as Digital First, which envision an all-digital future, or other approaches in which one delivery method is privileged over others.

Roger Fidler's *Mediamorphosis* situates media within an interdependent system, arguing against media displacement theories such as Digital First. He contends that "new media are not widely adapted on the merits of technology alone" but are dependent on social, political, and/or economic factors (1997, 29). Additionally, Fidler describes the contemporary media landscape as one in which "new media do not arise spontaneously and independently—they emerge gradually from the metamorphosis of old media. . . . [W]hen newer forms of communication emerge, the older forms usually do not die—they continue to evolve and adapt" (23).

In 2013 Iris Chyi's book on U.S. newspapers, *Trial and Error,* also debunked many of the myths underlying the Digital-First initiatives, including the myth that print is dying and that it is being displaced by online platforms. She contends that news executives have been misled by the disruptive innovation theory of Christensen and the advice of others who envision an all-digital future. Her research findings indicate that print "still outperforms the (supposedly hopeful) digital product by almost every standard, be it readership, engagement, advertising revenue, or paying intent" (10). In addition, the expectation that online advertising will be lucrative ignores the reality of the highly competitive online environment that includes free advertising on sites such as Craigslist and the vast array of news sources, including radio and television news sites, social media sites, and news aggregator sites.

Chyi also debunks the myth that it is not necessary for newspapers to do market research because the all-digital future will involve a new market consisting mostly of younger readers. Her findings indicate that online audiences are typically print subscribers who go online for breaking news, using newspaper websites as complements to print editions rather than as substitutes for print. Additionally, Chyi's readership research indicates audiences consider online platforms inferior to print because of factors such as eyestrain, intrusive advertising, and lower-quality content because the speed of posting content has taken priority over accuracy and balanced sourcing. Chyi advises the management of metro dailies to acknowledge that print does not have to die if they are willing to invest in it and to develop long-term strategies emphasizing content exclusivity and quality local coverage across platforms (2013). Chyi and Tenenboim's 2017 article reinforces this research with its study of more than fifty metro dailies (detailed previously). It provides evidence that newspaper penetration is still much greater than online penetration across local markets and that print readers are more likely to use newspaper sites than digital-only readers.

Scholar and former Canadian journalist Marc Edge also exposes myths about the demise of newspapers in his book *Greatly Exaggerated: The Myth of the Death of Newspapers* (2014a). Edge questions the assumption that newspapers are no longer profitable, a common rationale for staff reductions. Utilizing the 2006–2013 annual reports of several publicly traded U.S. and Canadian newspapers, Edge argues that, despite their financial losses and the widespread perception that they are on the verge of extinction, all of the newspapers in his study continued to make profits annually even when they were under Chapter 11 bankruptcy protection. Edge argues that, even during the recession, "newspapers weren't dying. Newspaper competition was. It was a trend that had been seen for decades and the financial crisis and high-speed Internet simply accelerated the trend" (9). In fact, he found that during the recession, newspapers were still profitable, and, since that time, they have averaged double-digit profits, a percentage that supersedes the 4.7 percent profit margin that *Fortune 500* companies typically average (Edge 2014b, 70).

Despite this research to the contrary, the myth persists that newspapers are dying, which Edge attributes to both "historical amnesia" and a lack of understanding of financial analysis (2014a, 224–225). Edge cites several examples of newspaper death narratives that appeared when new technologies emerged, starting with radio, then television, and then the Internet. Edge's book indicates newspapers were profitable, and although the recession accelerated declines in advertising and circulation that had begun decades earlier, "no major U.S. daily newspaper has closed since 2009" (Edge 2014a, 224–225). Further, those that closed were typically struggling second-place dailies in metro markets that could no longer sustain more than one daily (Edge 2014a, 2014b).

Edge's research complements that of Stephen Lacy, Michael Stamm, and Hugh Martin, who also criticize newspaper management for their cost-containment policies for short-term profitability. These policies, and the resulting increases in advertising prices as circulation continued to decline, "and expansion strategies all played significant roles in the creation of the current crisis" (Lacy, Stamm, and Martin 2014).

This criticism of newspapers for emphasizing profit over quality journalism was echoed in Philip Meyer's 2009 book, *The Vanishing Newspaper: Saving Journalism in the Information Age.* Meyer's research provides solid evidence of the correlation between quality journalism and newspaper profits and the need to reverse the deterioration of newspaper content due to divestment in print operations (2009). His work explains the historical context for the "easy-money culture" of the newspaper industry in the late 1990s, which saw average profit margins of 20 percent to 40 percent (Meyer 1995). These high margins enticed corporations to embark on acquisition sprees that eventually led to the overwhelming debt loads contributing to the industry's current crisis (Meyer 2009).

Although not specifically dedicated to metro dailies or the newspaper industry in general, Angela Phillips's 2014 book, *Journalism in Context,* elaborates on the crises facing not only newspapers but also journalism in general. It provides insight into the U.S. and European newspaper industries and their slow transition to multiplatform delivery. Phillips highlights the toll this process has taken on reduced newsroom staffs, not only in personal terms but also in terms of journalistic autonomy. Multiplatform delivery means less time and fewer resources for investigative and public service journalism as imperatives for continuous postings online, the emphasis on metrics (or audience clicks), and the time-consuming multimedia demands of the Internet take precedence.

Case Studies and Ethnographies

Often utilizing case studies and ethnographies to explain why the transition to multiplatform delivery has been so gradual, a number of journal articles have detailed the challenges of continually integrating new newsroom practices with traditional practices (Singer 2004; Avilés and Carvajal 2008; Carvajal and Avilés 2008; O'Sullivan and Heinonen 2008; Domingo 2008a; Paterson and Domingo 2008; Domingo and Paterson 2011). Among the common obstacles are the lack of time and resources for multimedia training, the rigidity and habitual nature of news routines, the lack of integration of online and print operations, and the lack of integration between editorial and information technology staffs (Deuze 2004; Domingo, 2008a, 2008b; Avilés and Carvajal 2008; Carvajal and Avilés 2008; Witschge and Nygren 2009; Robinson 2011; Ryfe 2012; Phillips 2014; Doyle 2015; Lischka 2015).

Additionally, the literature on newspapers depicts a disrupted media landscape in which there is less time for in-depth and investigative work and in which journalists increasingly lack autonomy as they are constantly pressured to post stories online as well as create videos, photo galleries, and slideshows (Gade and Perry 2003; Singer 2004; Avilés and Carvajal 2008; O'Sullivan and Heinonen 2008; Paterson and Domingo 2008; Witschge and Nygren 2009; Domingo and Paterson 2011; Lee-Wright, Phillips, and Witschge 2011; Ryfe 2012; M. Anderson 2013; Phillips 2014; Doyle 2015; Lischka 2015).

Although some early studies of newsrooms have taken a technologically deterministic approach by emphasizing the *effects* of technological innovation, this book takes a social-constructivist approach (or socially driven approach) to innovation utilized by several scholars detailed in *Making Online News* (Paterson and Domingo 2008; Domingo and Paterson 2011). This approach examines the actual *process* of adopting new technologies while addressing the distinctive social structures of different newsrooms (Paterson and Domingo 2008; Domingo and Paterson 2011; Ryfe 2012; Phillips 2014; Chyi 2013).

Case studies and ethnographic studies have been invaluable for providing insight into changing newsroom practices and newsroom culture. David Ryfe's 2012 book, *Can Journalism Survive?,* which utilizes ethnographies of three mid-sized regional daily newspapers in the early phase of their transitions to multiplatform news work, is particularly valuable. This study foregrounds many obstacles to changing newsroom practices, including the lack of training for multiplatform delivery, journalistic bias against online delivery, and the general printcentric journalistic culture that has dominated their norms and work routines. Ryfe finds that many staff members were unable to accord complementary status to both print and online news work. At one daily, he notes that the Internet was "still perceived as a 'black hole,' a place where quality journalism went to die" (2012, 103).

Sociologist Pablo Boczkowski also utilizes case studies and ethnographic methods to analyze U.S. online news operations and several South American newspapers as they transitioned to multiplatform delivery. His research describes the difficulty in integrating innovations into news practices, their loss of content diversity, and their reduced watchdog role over government (2004, 2010).

Nikki Usher's *Making News at* The New York Times is a contemporary history of the world-famous daily and its evolving newsroom, and the story of how journalists were caught "between tradition and change" in 2010 (2014a, 5). Although the layoffs and buyouts at the *Times* were relatively small compared to those at the average metro daily, its staff faced similar challenges in integrating print and online practices and in incorporating traditional and new media values (Walters 2017). Significantly, this book documents the printcentric biases that persisted even after the newsroom unified the print and online operations as well as the loss of institutional memory caused by newsroom buyouts in 2013.

Another valuable ethnography-based contribution to metro daily literature is C. W. Anderson's 2013 book, *Rebuilding the News.* It focuses on the Philadelphia news "ecosystem" in 2008 and details the relationships between the city's metro dailies, blogs, and independent media operations. This study is significant in foregrounding the growth of metrics (the measurement of reader preferences through mouse clicks) as they gained influence over story assignments and page layouts (C. Anderson 2011, 2013).

Overall, *Metro Dailies in the Age of Multimedia Journalism* is aimed at building on the small body of literature on metro dailies by examining a variety of metro dailies at a later and more advanced phase of their multiplatform transition. This current phase is characterized by practices and routines that are more established than in earlier newspaper research studies yet are still marked by experimentation and continual challenges in integrating print and online practices.

Methodology

The questions driving this study include the following: How and why are newspapers surviving despite so many being endangered and the predictions that they are on the verge of extinction? How have they transitioned from print only to both print and online/multimedia? What are metro dailies doing to reverse their declines in readership and profits?

In order to address these questions, I have relied on in-depth interviews, the interpretation of both scholarly and industry literature, and analyses of a variety of metro dailies and their news sites. A substantial portion of this book is based on the case studies of five metro newsrooms in five cities. This study was undertaken because in the last decade between twenty-five and thirty metro dailies have been periodically listed as endangered in news articles and in blogs by media analysts. I contacted ten of those metro dailies, and five agreed to participate in this project: the *Buffalo News,* the *Pittsburgh Post-Gazette,* the *Cleveland Plain Dealer,* the *St. Paul Pioneer Press,* and the *Minneapolis Star Tribune.*

Two of the cases in this book—the *Cleveland Plain Dealer* and the *Minneapolis Star Tribune*—are dailies that appeared on *Time* magazine's "10 Endangered Newspapers" list in 2009

(McIntyre 2009), and one, the *St. Paul Pioneer Press,* appeared on the 2014 "Top 10 Newspapers in Trouble" list (Real Clear Politics 2014). Much of the material that forms the book's newsroom narratives was drawn from ongoing in-depth interviews with more than forty experienced professionals beginning in 2013. The professionals were contacted via the snowball sampling method in which interviewees recommend future interview subjects. The interviews were conducted on the telephone and sometimes during newsroom visits. Most of them were digitally recorded. I had the opportunity to spend a day at each of the newsrooms, during which time I met with staff members, observed their interactions, attended meetings, conducted interviews, and documented their operations in still photography.

The material from the in-depth interviews provides a great deal of insight into the effects of the industry's changes on professionals currently working at metro dailies. Despite the fact that the industry is in flux and that the newspapers in this book each have distinctive histories, with each utilizing a variety of survival strategies, their case studies can provide an understanding of challenges and opportunities emerging in the age of multimedia journalism.

Although the emphasis in this Introduction thus far has been the newspaper crisis, this research also begs the question of why the industry has survived. One reason is that more readers still prefer print, despite the fact that a growing number of people are consuming news online (Barthel 2016). As previously detailed, the American Press Institute reported 71 percent of newspaper subscribers prefer print (Media Insight Project 2018).

Another reason for the survival of newspapers is the resiliency of their staffs in accommodating multiplatform delivery (Edge 2014a, 2014b; Phillips 2014; Doyle 2013). In addition, Edge attributes the survival of many newspapers to a "loyal readership that is highly prized by advertisers because it's educated, affluent and engaged" (2014a, 233). In light of this resiliency, *Metro Dailies* examines the strategies of several newspapers as they explore ways to engage these readers while experimenting with new revenue streams to face the current industry crisis.

Chapter Summaries

With the goal of presenting a contemporary history of several metro dailies, this book also aims to provide an inside perspective on newsroom changes, as professionals face not only financial challenges but also adaptation to the demands of multimedia and multiple platforms with fewer resources. Among the most salient challenges addressed in this book are continually changing technology and evolving practices, journalistic autonomy, union representation, monetizing online advertising, metrics, newsroom configurations, social media, and citizen journalism. This book also emphasizes the visual aspects of multimedia journalism, since photojournalism is central to both online and traditional newspapers yet often receives only cursory attention in most accounts of the newspaper industry.

In order to focus on the centrality of visual journalism to multimedia journalism, *Metro Dailies* begins with two overview chapters on how multimedia journalism and technological innovations have changed the newspaper industry. They underscore my key argument that a commitment to visual journalism across all platforms is necessary for a successful multiplatform approach to content delivery. These chapters also accentuate the necessity of retraining staffs in multimedia skills for online delivery and integrating new and established practices as well as highlighting issues such the blurring of the lines between professionals and nonprofessionals in the wake of citizen journalism, the Internet, and smartphone technology. Despite new online opportunities for professionals that include photo galleries, videos, and slideshows, the number of photojournalists who have been laid off has been much greater than the layoffs of reporters and editors. And while a common rationale is that photojournalists can be replaced by reporters with iPhones and citizen journalists, Chapter 2 contends that a commitment to professional photojournalism is still essential to multimedia journalism and that amateur photography cannot provide an adequate substitute for professional work.

The next three chapters present case studies of metro dailies. Chapter 3 focuses on the *Cleveland Plain Dealer*'s rapid implementation of the Digital-First strategy by the newspaper's parent corporation, Advance Publications. This involved massive layoffs and the division of the staff into three separate newsrooms as digital journalism was given priority over print. It also foregrounds the tension that erupted as the newsroom's culture dissolved and a greatly reduced staff struggled to maintain quality standards. This chapter argues that such Digital-First strategies devalue the print product by envisioning an all-digital future.

Chapter 4, on two metro dailies, the *Pittsburgh Post-Gazette* and the *Buffalo News,* examines more moderate yet differing approaches to multiplatform delivery. The *Pittsburgh Post-Gazette* has gradually implemented an integrated multiplatform approach, while the *Buffalo News* has moved from a printcentric approach to a Digital-First, print-secondary approach. Chapter 5, on the Minneapolis and St. Paul, Minnesota, newspapers, highlights the Twin Cities, one of the few metro areas still served by two metro dailies. It explains how the *Minneapolis Star Tribune* has emerged from bankruptcy and is thriving under the patronage of a civic benefactor. This newspaper exemplifies an integrated multiplatform delivery approach and a firm commitment to visual journalism across platforms. In contrast, this chapter also details how the *St. Paul Pioneer Press* is in decline, having been "harvested" or cost-cut by venture capitalist owners. The result has been a drastic reduction in not only its staff but also its coverage area, which no longer includes Minneapolis and is limited to a few counties in the St. Paul area.

The Conclusion presents some of the alternatives to corporate ownership, with examples of civic benefactors who have saved some newspapers on the brink of demise as well as examples of newspapers that have moved into the nonprofit sector. It looks at future directions for the newspaper industry as well as how some metro dailies are experimenting with nontraditional revenue-generating strategies that include utilizing their brands to provide marketing services and to sponsor events, and even offer novel services such as branded home cooking kits.

Overall these chapters are aimed at examining the status of some of the "endangered" metropolitan dailies during this period of crisis and rapid change as they slowly transition to multiplatform delivery and adapt their newsroom cultures and profitability strategies to the twenty-first century's dynamic media landscape. A key argument throughout is that there is a future for newspapers as long as newspaper companies are willing to integrate their print and online operations, make a commitment to visual journalism across platforms, make a commitment to journalistic integrity and autonomy, and retain staffs substantial enough to allow for quality content. At a time when the Trump administration has launched continuous assaults on media credibility and the media's vital role in speaking truth to power, it is in our best interest to see that newspapers survive in order to continue their public service roles so critical to our democracy.

1

Newspapers and Multimedia Journalism

The Challenges of Technological Change

Often overlooked in scholarly and industry literature has been the importance of newsroom reconfigurations in facilitating multiplatform delivery. One of the leaders in newsroom redesign has been the *Pittsburgh Post-Gazette.* In the summer of 2015, the *Post-Gazette*'s newsroom was moved from downtown to the north side of town. Its new leased space was custom-designed in an open-plan arrangement with a hub that centrally located the newspaper's multimedia news editors. The new newsroom also featured "clean sight lines and plenty of light" along with spectacular views, especially when compared to its historic offices where newspapers had been produced since 1927 (Coester 2017). In a newsroom-design report by the American Press Institute, executive editor David Shribman bluntly compared the two venues: "We wanted more light and less vermin. . . . We had the worst newsroom in history—old building, no windows, divided up into little warrens because of weight-bearing walls," Shribman said. "It wasn't conducive to anything. Ugly, dirty, depressing" (quoted in Coester 2017).

The *Post-Gazette*'s new design was so important in advancing the newspaper's multiplatform strategy that, well in advance of the move, Shribman had hired the architect who had designed

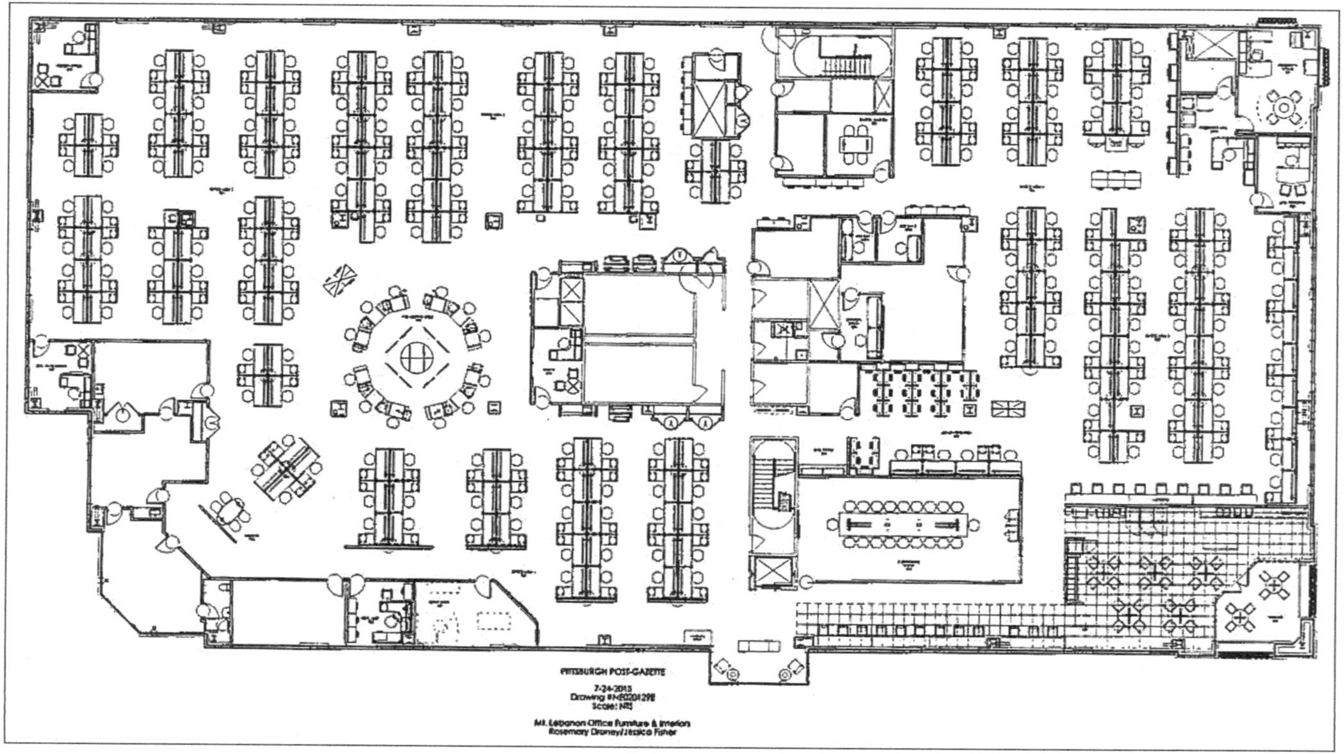

Shown here is the blueprint for the *Pittsburgh Post-Gazette* multimedia newsroom. (Photo courtesy of the *Pittsburgh Post-Gazette*.)

the *Toronto Globe and Mail*'s newsroom (Shribman interview, August 8, 2015). The *Post-Gazette*'s open floor plan was intended to facilitate collaborations and multiplatform delivery, with TVs hanging from the ceiling that constantly call attention to the latest news. The newsroom also has a photo and video studio, and temporary workspaces called "hotel seating" (*Pittsburgh Post-Gazette* 2014; Shribman interviews, August 8, 2015, and October 21, 2016).

The *Post-Gazette* is one of many metros that have relocated in recent years from expensive venues in the heart of a city to cheaper venues redesigned to accommodate scaled-down news staffs and to emphasize multiplatform delivery (Usher 2013, 2014b, 2015). Although there is no standard design plan for these new newsrooms, they commonly include open plan spaces without cubicles, a centrally located editing hub, large amounts of natural lighting, and televisions mounted on walls or hung from ceilings (Coester 2017; Usher 2013, 2015). According to a study on the relocation of metro daily newsrooms, Nikki Usher found that the hub was an important indicator of how multiplatform delivery has changed newsroom practices:

> The creation of news hubs offers insight into the industry-wide approach to thinking about digital workflow. What we see is a physical effort to make it easier to cover breaking news. This idea of where to arrange desks might be quickly dismissed as another newsroom fad. But even if it is a fad, it signifies a very explicit attempt to reorient newsroom priorities. . . . The hub brings together the key players for online news distribution—some combination of homepage producers, metro editors, photo assignment editors and social media specialists. (Usher 2014b, 58–59)

Televisions are also major components of newsroom redesigns, representing the emphasis on breaking news. All five of the subjects of the case studies in this book had televisions hanging prominently in their newsrooms. After the introduction of broadcast news, but prior to the Internet, metro dailies had developed reputations for long-form stories and investigative reportage, while radio and then television became the primary sources for breaking news (Phillips 2014; Waldman 2011; Lee-Wright, Phillips, and Witschge 2011). But since the introduction of the Internet, the competition for breaking news not only has expanded to newspaper websites but also has attracted radio, television, and a new array of news providers, from aggregators such as *Google News* to digital-only operations such as the *Huffington Post.* And while covering breaking news has been facilitated by multimedia technology, there is serious concern expressed in scholarly and professional literature and by my interviewees that the increasing emphasis on breaking news has not come without a steep price. Breaking news has spawned an obsession with immediacy and scooping one's competitors and leaves little time for even the essentials such as thorough editing and the vetting of sources let alone for time-consuming long-form and investigative stories (Starkman 2014; Phillips 2014; Lee-Wright, Phillips, and Witschge 2011; Waldman 2011). This literature also emphasizes the problem of metrics determining story assignments or layout priorities.

While concern for the overemphasis on metrics was not prominent in my interviews with the *Post-Gazette* staff, this was a major concern for several staff members at the *Cleveland Plain Dealer* (as is detailed in Chapter 3). They complained about daily quotas for online postings and management's emphasis on stories that attracted the most hits. This not only undercuts journalistic autonomy but also introduces a competitive ethos to the newsroom and puts a premium on stories that generate hits over stories on government and society that fulfill the newspaper's public service role.

Integrating Online and Print Platforms

In describing the innovative design of the *Post-Gazette*'s newsroom, Shribman noted that it was intended to integrate print and digital production practices and to promote collaboration across units (Shribman interviews, August 8, 2015, and October 21, 2016). Significantly, Shribman said he believed the *Pittsburgh Post-Gazette* has

> moved from an antediluvian, atomized, horrific work site to the most modern newsroom in the United States designed specifically to promote convergence, cross pollination, technological innovation. This was not a mistake or a coincidence. It was a deliberate decision to change the place where we work to reflect the place we have to be in the modern society. (Shribman interview, August 8, 2015)

Shribman added that the success of the newsroom design was evident soon after moving into the new space.

> I was just saying . . . look what's happening here in this newsroom that didn't happen a month ago: people are sitting and talking—people who you never see together . . . somebody born, I'm guessing, in probably the Truman years sitting with someone who experienced the end of the Cold War first-hand in Kazakhstan. That's because our old building was lots of little rooms; this [arrangement] is a whole different thing . . . and the metaphor is the horizon. We can see the far horizon from here. (Shribman interview, August 8, 2015)

In a 2017 American Press Institute report on newsroom design, Shribman noted that the *Post-Gazette*'s open space and extensive amount of natural light also reflected a concern for staff morale. "We're in a financially distressed industry trying to find some oxygen," he said (quoted in Coester 2017). To Shribman, the *Pittsburgh Post-Gazette*'s design expresses a sense of optimism and an emphasis on looking toward the future (Coester 2017). This sense of optimism evoked by innovative design is also highlighted in Usher's research on metros that have moved out of their old centrally located flagship buildings in downtown areas to redesigned, less-centralized leased spaces (Usher 2014b, 2015). Usher's work and research by Dana Coester reveal that new newsrooms can be morale boosters simply because a shrinking staff no longer has to face rows of empty desks in dingy newsrooms designed for groups that were 30 to 50 percent larger (Coester 2017; Usher 2014b, 2015).

On the other hand, Usher's work also describes the down side to these moves, as the staff relocates from buildings owned by the newspapers, their brand names boldly emblazoned on their façades, to less-prominent leased spaces in buildings shared with other businesses (Usher 2014b, 2015). "To some journalists, leaving the mothership behind does indeed represent loss and a significant break with the past" (Usher 2014b, 5).

Newsrooms Persist despite "Backpack Journalism"

The concept of setting aside workspaces for temporary use or "hoteling," a feature included in the *Post-Gazette*'s newsroom redesign, allows for individuals who work primarily from the field to occasionally use newsroom space. This concept of temporary, depersonalized workspaces in the newsroom works well for staff members who work remotely as the ability to work from the field has increased with the availability of cell phones and laptops. Such technologies have enabled the development of what's called "backpack journalism." These are "digital one-man bands" in which reporters work from the field, not only writing stories but also shooting, editing, and transmitting video and photos to the newsroom (Shister 2010). However, there is a question of whether multimedia journalism should be done by individuals in the field or by teams headquartered in the newsroom.

As Angela Phillips (2014) has noted in *Journalism in Context,* although technology has enabled one-man bands, this is very difficult to do well because it draws on different aspects of a person's attention. The result is often mediocre and low-quality content. To Martha Stone, CEO of World Newsmedia Network, much of what is produced by backpack journalists is "a mush of mediocrity" because such journalism requires a journalist to be a "jack of all trades" (Stone 2002). This is echoed by Lou Ureneck, the chairman of Boston University's journalism department, who emphasized that "being a reporter is a fully engaging task," and who compared backpack journalism to "driving and trying to read a map" (quoted in Shister 2010). Gary Kebbel, editorial director of America Online, expressed similar views: "I also resist the notion of backpack journalists because I believe it is being foisted on us by publishers who don't feel that 20% profit is good enough. I think they are simply trying to eliminate jobs" (quoted in Stone 2002). This is a convincing argument given the number of layoffs in the industry since the turn of the twenty-first century. Further, Stone's article emphasizes the need to use backpack journalists only occasionally, recommending that newspapers invest in multimedia production teams to routinely do this work, especially for breaking news stories (Stone 2002).

The emergence of backpack journalism has also sparked predictions that remote journalism might eventually eliminate the need for a newsroom (Usher 2014b, 2015; Washeck 2014). However, many journalists have found that backpack journalism is challenging not only in perceptual terms but also in terms of establishing work routines and keeping up with the best practices in multimedia journalism. Usher's and Coester's studies, among others, highlight the "physical relevance" of newsrooms because they fulfill the need for regular places to write and edit as well as provide video studio facilities (Coester 2017; Usher 2014b, 2015). Less tangible, but nonetheless very significant, are the social factors that make the newsroom viable, including the accessibility of colleagues for advice as well as for inspiration and stimulation (Coester 2017; Usher 2014b, 2015). According to Usher:

> Journalists still imagine what they do to be part of a greater whole. They privilege face-to-face relationships as a way to work out stories, trade tidbits of information, and gossip. While they can and do work from home, most journalists still find value in coming to a set, physical place. This makes the physical location of the news-

> room important as proximity to sources and home base facilitates their work. Physical roots remain important for human relations inside and outside the newsroom. (2014b, 60)

Literature on Newsroom Redesigns

As metro dailies across the country have reconfigured their newsrooms for multiplatform delivery, a body of literature has emerged on the relationship between media convergence and newsroom design (Paterson and Domingo 2008; Domingo and Patterson 2011; Usher 2013, 2015; Coester 2017). Generally, Coester's and Usher's work emphasizes how space affects morale, and how it facilitates collaboration and stimulates innovation (Coester 2017; Usher 2013, 2015). Besides open-plan configurations, many newsroom designs also include experimental fluid or unassigned spaces that offer individuals or groups a change of environment to facilitate their productivity (Coester 2017; Usher 2014b, 2015).

Scholars increasingly emphasize that true integration of print and online work practices requires not only changing physical spaces but also restructuring newsrooms to include multimedia teams and news desks that centralize multiplatform delivery, which are also features of the *Pittsburgh Post-Gazette*'s new newsroom (Lischka 2015; Carvajal and Avilés 2008; Bressers 2006). Notably, Bonnie Bressers's 2006 study of more than fifty U.S. metro dailies argues that the proximity between departments afforded by hub designs is not enough to ensure multiplatform integration and that a newsroom should include a converged news desk to coordinate cross-platform work. At the time of her study very few metros had established converged news desks, but in recent years these have become more common (Coester 2017).

However, not all of the literature argues for the efficacy of hubs with centralized multimedia news desks. In *Making Online News*, Anja Bechmann rejects the centralization of converged news desks, or "superdesks," on the basis of her study of Danish cross-media news organizations. Instead she advocates decentralizing newsroom configurations and rearranging them to facilitate collaborations between "networks of interest" to achieve multiplatform integration (2011, 18). Christopher Paterson's 2011 study of international news services Reuters and AP also expresses doubt about the effectiveness of hubs in facilitating collaboration when so much of the communication among staffers is typically through instant messaging and e-mail.

In terms of multiplatform delivery, some scholars have argued that a key obstacle to integration of print and digital platforms is the unequal status given to online journalism. Bressers's study found that many staff members were still resistant to online work because they perceived online as inferior to print. David Ryfe's 2004–2009 study of regional daily newspapers as they transitioned into multiplatform news also highlights this printcentric bias (Ryfe 2012; Carvajal and Avilés 2008; Bressers 2006). Bressers (2006) argues that, because of this bias, successful multiplatform integration made it necessary for newspapers to equalize the status of online and print work and encourage their print-side staffs to produce exclusive website content.

And while Iris Chyi's (2013) research also focuses on multiplatform delivery, she disagrees with this notion that newspapers should equalize the status of print and online news because readership and metro daily studies indicate that online news is generally considered inferior to print. In an article reporting the results of their multiyear study of fifty U.S. metro dailies that concluded in 2015, Chyi and Ori Tenenboim detail the "performance gap" between print and online products and maintain that although readers used digital platforms, they still preferred print. Further, these researchers found that print "surpassed online reach by a wide margin across all age groups" (Chyi and Tenenboim 2017).

Chyi (2013) argues that digital platforms are considered inferior generally because of retinal fatigue from staring at light-emitting screens, annoying pop-up ads, and the frequent inaccuracies, as speed in posting content is given precedence over accuracy and balance. In addition, Chyi points out that findings from psychological studies repeatedly showed "human brains prefer tangible media" (2013, 81). Consequently, reading styles vary with the platform, with people generally scanning digital content, while reading more slowly, with greater comprehension, in print. "One study after another has revealed that news in print generates better recall than news in digital formats" (Chyi 2013, 81). This is borne out in eye-track studies of both print and digital platforms, with equipment measuring eye movements to determine what elements on a particular page attracted viewers and how long they were engaged in viewing them (Holmqvist et al. 2003). Generally, this research describes a complementary relationship between print and digital news consumption, with people frequently scanning online in short sessions for breaking news while reading more slowly and for longer periods for the detailed coverage provided by print (S. Quinn 2007).

Consequently, contrary to what Digital-First advocates typically assert, Chyi argues convincingly that digital platforms should be seen as complementary to print rather than as the successors to print (2013, 80). Chyi elaborates on her argument using what she calls her "Ramen Noodle Theory." This posits that inferior goods will be used for specific functions such as checking online for breaking news. However, news executives should "consider how people consume ramen noodles or fast food—they use inferior goods when they need to, when normal goods are not as readily available or affordable. And many inferior goods are profitable, too. One thing is for sure though: Ramen noodles should not be marketed as steak" (82).

Visual Journalism's Significance across Platforms

Although the debate continues about the status of print versus digital platforms, it is important to note that, regardless of the platform, studies indicate visuals are the most powerful components of both online and print pages (S. Quinn 2007). Visual journalism not only attracts readers and draws their eyes to headlines and stories; it also boosts story completion rates (Fisher 2015; Moses 2002). In addition, studies show that larger news photographs on social media sites attract more readers and engage them for longer periods of time (Ulloa et al. 2015; Kitschke 2017).

In addition to the literature on visual journalism, in-depth interviews for this book and recent eye-tracking studies emphasize that photos, photo galleries, and slideshows have favorable metrics, while videos are less popular, especially with older populations such as a large segment of the readers of the *Buffalo News* (detailed in Chapter 4 herein; see also S. Quinn 2015). While most metro dailies studied in this book do not typically post a large number of videos on a daily basis, many periodically include videos in multimedia story packages with photos, stories, and video all related to a specific topic. In recent years the larger metros have been emphasizing video, with both the *New York Times* and the *Washington Post* adding visual journalists to their staffs. In 2017 the *Times* announced plans to hire about twelve "visual-first journalists" who are expert in reporting in both still photography and video (Montgomery 2017; Benton 2017; Lichterman 2017).

You Can't Do More with Fewer People

In a 2011 FCC report on the U.S. media landscape, researcher Steven Waldman (2011) details many aspects of coverage that have been lost as reduced newspaper staffs have been expected to assume multimedia workloads with very little training in visual journalism and as the emphasis has moved from in-depth, well-vetted, well-balanced news stories to short paragraphs updated frequently but often posted before a story is fully vetted and edited. What's been diminished or eliminated varies from metro to metro, but this frequently includes coverage of health, education, state government, and local government (Reinardy 2016; Shapiro, Hiatt, and Hoyt 2015; Edge 2014a; Phillips 2014; Waldman 2011). Although the large staffs of metro dailies have been best equipped for investigative work, and this work has earned many metros national reputations, staff cutbacks and the demands of multimedia reporting in the twenty-first century have led to the elimination or reduction of investigative reporters and teams at metros across the country (Reinardy 2016; Starkman 2014; Phillips 2014; Lee-Wright, Phillips, and Witschge 2011; Waldman 2011). Waldman articulates well what's been lost in the newspaper industry:

> Experts tell us that these days, much of reporters' time is taken up on reactive stories, describing what happened on a more superficial level, rather than digging deep into the causes and implications of a development. They have less time to investigate, to question, to take a story to the next level. Fewer newsrooms than ever can afford to deploy reporters to work on labor-intensive stories. That means not only fewer investigative stories, but also, more commonly, less daily beat reporting about municipal government, schools, the environment, local businesses, and other topics that impact Americans' future, safety, livelihood, and everyday life. In very real ways, the dramatic newspaper-industry cutbacks appear to have caused genuine harm to American citizens and local communities. (2011, 57)

Dean Starkman's book *The Watchdog That Didn't Bark* blames the disappearance of investigative journalism on a combination of the newspaper crisis, digital technology, and corporate antipathy to "accountability journalism" (2014, 8). According to Starkman:

> It has been unnerving to witness how the Internet's strengths—limitless space, a 24/7 publishing schedule, precise quantity and popularity metrics—have meshed with old-fashioned corporate imperatives of sped-up reporter productivity and indifferent journalism quality. High-flown rhetoric of futuristic digitism is deployed . . .

to justify reckless and unnecessary cost cuts in regional newsrooms and to marginalize reporting in the public interest. (15)

Starkman warns of the "destructive" capabilities of strategies such as Digital First that stress brief entertainment stories over the investigative stories that fulfill a newspaper's public service role (2014). Chapter 3 herein details the destructiveness of the Digital-First imperative at the *Cleveland Plain Dealer* as journalistic autonomy decreased and time for investigative work became extremely limited. A particularly illustrative example involves investigative reporter Rachel Dissell, who is foregrounded in Chapter 3. From the early 2000s until 2014, Dissell had worked the courts beat. During that time, her investigative work won awards and was a catalyst for legislation ameliorating the state's neglect of DNA testing of rape kits (Dissell interview). In 2013 the *Plain Dealer*'s parent company, Advance Publications, launched its Digital-First imperative by laying off approximately one-third of the newsroom. In 2014 Advance restructured the newsroom, reassigning several beat reporters, including Dissell, to an "enterprise" team that was expected to generate original reporting on crime, the courts, government corruption, and social justice (Clark 2014a). Priority was given to frequent daily online postings and to producing multimedia packages with stories, still photos, and videos, making long-term investigative journalism a distant second (Dissell interview).

Although Dissell said she believed it is important to get stories out on multiple platforms, she found visual journalism challenging. While she said she took pride in some of her multimedia work, especially the video and photos she produced for her story on house flipping, Dissell said generally she found it very difficult to move between writing and visual journalism (Dissell interview). Back in 2002 this problem was highlighted by the recommendations of multimedia journalist Jane Stevens, who wrote that because true backpack journalists are rare, multimedia journalism should be practiced by teams rather than by individuals (Stevens 2002).

Conclusion

This chapter has emphasized the revolutionary changes in newspapers as a result of multiplatform delivery and how this has impacted every facet of the industry from newsroom design and structure to technology and practices. In terms of newsroom design, current configurations, such as open floor plans, hubs, and fluid spaces, generally reflect the integration of print and online units and the emphasis on collaboration and innovation between teams, editors, and different departments. Newsroom designs also emphasize the importance of breaking news and digital delivery through televisions prominently displaying the latest news or real-time analytics from newspapers' websites.

Notably, while redesigned newsrooms can facilitate multiplatform delivery, they are ineffective without a newsroom culture in which journalists feel empowered to work autonomously, free from the corporate emphasis on individual article metrics, on daily story quotas, and on backpack journalism. This chapter also asserts that, in most cases, multimedia news work is best practiced by teams that coordinate content between newsrooms and the field rather than by jack-of-all-trades individuals working untethered from the newsroom. Teamwork also reinforces the viability of newsrooms because it requires regular workspaces and facilitates informational and social interactions with colleagues.

While the integration of print and online operations is a common goal for metro dailies, there is still debate about whether print and online platforms are accorded equal status by news consumers. While some scholars and experts believe people consume news the same way regardless of platform, Chyi and others have made powerful arguments that online and print platforms are used differently and online platforms are typically inferior because of conditions like retinal fatigue and the lower standards for online news than for print.

Also detailed in this chapter are some of the disadvantages of multiplatform delivery in an era of shrinking newsrooms and the difficulty journalists have in keeping up with the 24/7 demands of the Web while continuing with long-term and investigative journalism. In addition, it emphasizes how strategies such as Digital First have contributed to the decrease or elimination of investigative and long-form journalism.

Overall this chapter underscores this book's key argument that successful multiplatform delivery requires newspapers to make major commitments to integrating print and online practices and to emphasizing visual journalism both online and in print. As Chapter 2 shows, paradoxically, despite the significance of visual journalism to multiplatform delivery, photojournalists have been the most vulnerable to layoffs in metro dailies across the country.

2

Photojournalism

The Focal Point of Multimedia Journalism

Over the course of his career, *Chicago Sun-Times* photojournalist John White won numerous international awards, including a Pulitzer Prize in 1982. He also received the Sprague Award, the National Press Photographers Association's highest honor, and was awarded Photographer of the Year five times by the Chicago Press Photographers Association. White was described by a former *Sun-Times* managing editor as "the eye that was always looking for the soul of Chicago" (Irby 2013). Yet these exceptional credentials and more than thirty years on the newspaper's staff did not prevent him from being fired on May 30, 2013, along with twenty-seven other *Sun-Times* photojournalists (Mitchell 2013). The night before the layoffs, the photographers were alerted by e-mail about a mandatory staff meeting the next morning but were given no indication about why they would be meeting. The process was swift. After a short announcement that eliminated the photo staff, the photographers received their layoff packets, had their access badges demagnetized, and were told to turn in any equipment owned by the company. White described the meeting as "intimidating" and exuding a "toxic and unkind spirit" (quoted in Irby 2013). "It was as if they pushed a button and deleted a whole culture of photojournalism," he said.

The company's rationale for discarding its photo department was that the newspaper was "evolving" and would be offering more video content to meet the needs of its readers (Winslow 2013). Some staff members found this baffling, given the popularity of the newspaper's online photo galleries and the video skills of many of its photojournalists (Garcia 2013). Nonetheless, in the future the *Sun-Times* planned to rely on reporters with iPhones, citizen photojournalists, and freelancers for its visual journalism. Although the *Sun-Times* had been under bankruptcy protection since 2009 and had undergone numerous rounds of buyouts and layoffs, the elimination of the entire department came as a shock, especially since the company was in the midst of negotiations with the newspaper guild, which would have ensured that no photojournalists would be laid off (Associated Press 2013).

While the situation at the *Chicago Sun-Times* is one of the most drastic cases of layoffs in photojournalism, the statistics for the field are grim nonetheless. According to the American Society of News Editors annual survey, between the years 2000 and 2012, the number of photojournalist jobs in the United States was cut almost in half, amounting to a 43 percent reduction (M. Anderson 2013). This trend extended through 2014. It included thirteen photojournalists eliminated from the *Orlando Sentinel* in February 2014 and the loss of nine photojournalist and photo editor positions in July 2014 at the self-proclaimed "New York's Picture Newspaper," the *New York Daily News* (National Press Photographers Association 2014; Walker 2014). Although layoff statistics for 2015 and 2016 were unavailable, Donald Winslow, editor of the National Press Photographer Association's magazine, *News Photographer,* wrote that he was not aware of any large-scale layoffs during those years. "But from just my gut feeling, it feels like newspapers have 'sized' themselves to the point where now they're barely staffed and are operating in that shoestring manner" (Winslow interview). This is particularly true at the *St. Paul Pioneer Press,* as detailed in Chapter 5.

As these layoffs have continued, a growing number of media analysts and scholars have been predicting professional newspaper photojournalism is dying or has died (Britton 2012; Burgess 2010; Jolly 2009; Gillmor 2006a, 2009). They assume a technologically deterministic philosophy that attributes the demise of photojournalism to constantly improving digital technology. This position implies that technology enables anyone to take acceptable pictures and that the experience and training of professionals is insignificant. The evidence for this position often includes the increasing number of reporters taking iPhone photographs and the outsourcing of eyewitness disaster or crisis photos to citizen journalists or to freelancers (Zelizer 2007; Britton 2012).

Despite the drastic cuts in the ranks of newspaper photojournalists, there are other scholars and analysts who contend that layoffs should be seen within the context of a declining newspaper industry that is also laying off reporters, editors, graphic artists, and even some online staff members. They contend that photojournalists have been hit the hardest because their departments are the most expensive (Bailey 2013; Spinner 2013; Ryfe 2012; Huffaker 2013; Estrin 2010; Campbell 2010).

Statistics on reporters and editors from the American Society of News Editors survey cited above bear this out. Between the years 2000 and 2012, jobs for newspaper reporters and writers decreased by 32 percent, and jobs for copyeditors, layout editors, and online producers decreased by 27 percent (M. Anderson 2013).

While not often emphasized in the literature on photojournalism, another key reason the cutbacks have been so deep is the traditionally inferior position of photojournalists within newsroom hierarchies (Klein-Avraham and Reich 2016; Yaschur 2012; Lowrey 2002). Because writers typically dominate newsroom management, photojournalists are often regarded as technicians or button pushers rather than full-fledged journalists with cameras, and it is much easier to lay off staff members if they are seen as merely nonessential personnel (Klein-Avraham and Reich 2016; Yaschur 2012; Langton 2008; Lowrey 2002). According to Neal Lambert, team leader in the Photography Department of the *St. Paul Pioneer Press*, news photography has always suffered from reporters' perceptions that the photo staff is a "service department" that will provide illustrations for their stories (Lambert interview). Dave Orrick, government and politics reporter and former outdoors writer/photographer for the *St. Paul Pioneer Press,* echoed this view: "As a reporter who's become a photographer, it's much harder than reporters and editors think" (Orrick interview, May 18, 2015). Jim Gehrz, award-winning photojournalist formerly with the *Minneapolis Star Tribune,* said he does not expect the status of photojournalists to improve because management typically comprises word people who do not appreciate visual journalism. "Editors and reporters don't understand what you do. . . . [T]he iPhone has diluted people's perceptions of what's good. . . . Just because you buy a piano, doesn't make you Mozart" (Gehrz interview, June 30, 2015).

Adding to the status devaluation of the professional photojournalist is the blurring of the lines between professional and amateur, as digital technology has enabled amateurs to become eyewitnesses to news events and crises and have opportunities to publish on mainstream news sites or citizen media or social media sites (Allan 2013; Allan and Thorsen 2009; Andén-Papadopoulos and Pantti 2011, 2013; Mortensen and Keshelashvili 2013; Pantti and Bakker 2009).

Overall, this chapter situates the drastic cuts in the ranks of photojournalists within the context of the decline of the newspaper industry. It emphasizes the importance of photojournalism to both online and print platforms, reinforcing my key argument that an integrated multiplatform approach requires a substantial commitment to visual journalism in terms of the size of the staff and the amount of space across platforms that is allotted to images. I raise here a number of questions, including these: Why are the cutbacks of photojournalists so severe? How has professional photojournalism been affected by reporters with iPhones and citizen photojournalism? How have photojournalists adapted to the demands of both print and online platforms?

Despite the popularity of iPhone photography and photo sharing, I argue here that these practices are not evidence that professional photojournalists will be replaced by nonprofessionals. Rather, I contend that photo sharing is principally a social practice and photojournalism is an informational practice, and that amateurs are more interested in using photography for social and self-documentation purposes than for journalistic purposes (Allan 2013; Allan and Thorsen 2009; Andén-Papadopoulos and Pantti 2011, 2013; Cohen 2005; Murray 2008). Consequently, rather than attributing the layoffs of photojournalists to competition from citizen journalists, I argue that the major factors are both the high costs of photo departments and the inferior status of photojournalists, who are often regarded in the newsroom hierarchy as technicians rather than as trained visual journalists.

Conceptual Framework

Recent scholarship provides insight into the changes wrought by and the challenges of multimedia technology on the field of photojournalism, many of which are reflected in interviews with photojournalists for this study. In their research on Israeli photojournalists, Inbal Klein-Avraham and Zvi Reich (2016) examined photojournalism in light of technological innovations that have disrupted work practices. These innovations not only have brought new tools and venues for visual journalists but also have disrupted their norms and routines and blurred the lines between professionals and amateurs (Brüggemann et al. 2016; Doyle 2013, 2015; Lischka 2015) This research highlights how new technology and the availability of the Internet have decreased the distinctive role of professional photojournalists, further eroding their status within the newsroom hierarchy, and accounting in large part for their dispensability by newsroom management (Klein-Avraham and Reich 2016; Lowrey 2002).

As citizen photojournalism has become acceptable to the mainstream media, and in particular newspapers, the dominance of professional photojournalists has diminished (Andén-Papadopoulos and Pantti 2011; Mäenpää 2014; Mortensen and Keshelashvili 2013; Pantti and Bakker 2009). This has meant that eye witnessing, traditionally dominated by professionals, is now shared with amateurs, both reporters with iPhones and citizen journalists (Zelizer 2007; Andén-Papadopoulos and Pantti 2013; Allan and Thorsen 2009; Allan 2013; Pantti 2013). Yet recent studies have found professionals have conflicting attitudes about the growing acceptance of citizen photojournalism. On one hand, many appreciate the fact that citizens can now photograph in the midst of a crisis or disaster to complement professional work, yet many also express concern about the inability to verify citizen work and the possibilities of citizens staging photographs and manipulating their work with Photoshop. This ambiguity was reflected in many of my interviews with photojournalists at metro dailies. Typically, photojournalists were also concerned that the acceptance of the lower standard for citizen photojournalism would generally lower the technical and aesthetic standards for the field (Mortensen 2014; Mortensen and Keshelashvili 2013; Mäenpää 2014; Pantti 2013; Chan interview; DeYoung interview; Gehrz interview, March 25, 2013; Kordalski interview, March 20, 2016; Lambert interview; Orrick interview, May 18, 2015; Peterson interview).

Much has been written about the publication venues for citizen journalists that have been opened up on the Internet (Andén-Papadopoulos and Pantti 2011, 2013; Allan 2013; Singer et al. 2011; Allan and Thorsen 2009; Pantti and Bakker 2009; Gillmor 2006a, 2006b, 2009; Jenkins 2006). Henry Jenkins's work (2006) on participatory culture is particularly relevant for understanding the rise of citizen journalism in the twenty-first century, where previously audiences could act only as passive news consumers, rarely participating in news reporting and photojournalism. Jenkins describes citizen journalism (both photos and text) as a product of convergence culture. In this contemporary multimedia environment, it is now routine for mainstream media outlets to solicit from audiences not only comments but also visual and written news content, often referred to as "user-generated content." Yet the body of scholarly literature on participatory journalism, or news work by both professionals and nonprofessionals, frequently emphasizes the lack of collaboration between professionals and amateurs because of the persistence of traditional journalistic norms and values and professional control over editing and placement (Bruns 2005; Hermida and Thurman 2008; Domingo et al. 2008; Paulussen and Ugille 2008; Singer et al. 2011).

The Rise of Citizen Journalism

In 2011–2012 citizen journalism from the Middle East received a great deal of visibility in traditional and online media as photos, news stories, and personal accounts of antigovernment protests were smuggled to news outlets around the world despite government censorship efforts (Allan 2013; Andén-Papadopoulos and Pantti 2013). Yet, ironically, while the category of amateur crisis and disaster photography receives the most media attention, it is the area that makes the smallest contributions to mainstream media outlets (Pantti and Bakker 2009; Buehner 2011; Allan and Thorsen 2009; Monaghan and Tunney 2010). According to Kari Andén-Papadopoulos and Mervi Pantti, "A great majority of amateur images that are offered to news organizations are characterized by their *lack* of news value" (2011, 12). In their research on citizen journalists, Tara Mortensen and Ana Keshelashvili point out that "few citizens want to do the kind of journalism that news organizations demand and they are mainly interested in getting published by covering topics about which they are passionate" (2013, 147). Commonly, contributors post photographs of sunsets, weather shots, pets, families, and mundane images of everyday life (Andén-Papadopoulos and Pantti 2011; Pantti and Bakker 2009; Buehner 2011; Monaghan and Tunney 2010). Generally, scholars emphasize the difference in the perspectives of amateurs and professionals: Amateurs tend to view photography as "documentary proof" and usually favor the informal "snapshot" style of photography compared to photojournalists, who use a formal, carefully composed narrative style (Mortensen and Keshelashvili 2013; Cohen 2005; Murray 2008).

Although citizen photojournalists have contributed news images in relatively small quantities to mainstream news outlets, some scholars have detailed the "uneasy relationship" between journalists/photojournalists and amateurs that has led to defensiveness by professionals against the increasingly blurred lines between amateurs and professionals (Pantti 2013; Andén-Papadopoulos and Pantti 2013; Lewis, Kaufhold, and Lasorsa 2010; 2012; Singer et al. 2011; Hermida et al. 2011; Domingo et al. 2008; Hermida and Thurman 2008). In terms of the challenges citizen journalism might pose to professional photojournalism, as Andén-Papadopoulos and Pantti have pointed out, citizen involvement in journalism largely remains "within the framework and control of professional journalism" (2011, 12).

Nonetheless, eyewitness images of disasters and crises have been considered the most significant contributions by nonprofessionals, since gathering eyewitness evidence has long been considered a key journalistic practice (Zelizer 2007; Allan 2013). According to photojournalist Gehrz, this eye-witnessing role is important:

> I do believe that the proliferation of many additional voices/eyes to witness happenings in the world and report back is a good thing. With the advent of the Internet, not since Gutenberg have people been so empowered. In a way, the more people who share their knowledge about a given experience, the better, in that it serves as a check and balance to ensure that all media outlets must tell the truth. (Gehrz interview, June 30, 2015)

While Gehrz said he appreciated the diversity of voices that citizen photojournalism provides, he said that the *Minneapolis Star Tribune,* like many other U.S. metro dailies, has a sizeable enough staff and a large enough pool of professional freelancers that they rarely rely on citizen contributions unless there is a crisis situation (Gehrz interview, June 30, 2015).

The Newspaper Industry in Decline

To deal with the deteriorating economic conditions at many large newspapers, a common cost-cutting strategy has been to lay off staff members. As previously discussed, several analysts and scholars attribute the high number of layoffs of photojournalists to the high costs of maintaining photo departments. In reference to the case of the *Chicago Sun-Times,* Mike Zajakowski, picture editor for the *Chicago Tribune,* was quoted in a blog: "Photojournalism is expensive. . . . The equipment costs are staggering. Doing stories right often takes time, effort and planning. Maintaining a staff of professionals is a serious commitment" (Spinner 2013).

Further, some analysts have noted that the layoffs may have more to do with trying to break up the union stronghold while disguising these efforts as budget cuts. Newspapers can lay off full-time union photojournalists and rehire them as part-time non-union staff members without benefits (Irby 2013; Associated Press 2013; Bever 2013; Kirkland 2014). This was the cost-cutting strategy adopted in 2008 at *Newsday,* a daily paper that serves Long Island and is distributed throughout New York City. At that time, the former publisher, Timothy Knight, who later became president of cleveland.com, fired the entire photo staff, after which he moved on to become CEO for the *Sun-Times* (National Press Photographers Association 2008; Irby 2013; Associated Press 2013). At *Newsday,* after eliminating twenty full-time staff positions, Knight's administration subsequently invited laid-off photojournalists to apply for approximately seven positions as "visual journalists" (National Press Photographers Association 2008).

Cell-Phone versus High-Resolution Images

Although cell-phone cameras are convenient, their photos are typically low quality and cannot be enlarged without reducing the images to pixel patterns. In addition, their low-quality lenses are unable to capture critical detail, particularly for close-up and stop-action photography. In 2013, not long after the layoffs at the *Sun-Times,* the Chicago Blackhawks won the Stanley Cup. A comparison of front-page photographs of two of Chicago's major newspapers indicates the limits of iPhone photography.

The *Chicago Sun-Times* front page is dominated by graph-

CHICAGO SUN-TIMES.com

Hawks captain Jonathan Toews brings the Stanley Cup into The Scout bar early Tuesday.

CUP OF CHEER

COMPLETE COVERAGE OF STANLEY'S HOMECOMING INSIDE

This *Chicago Sun-Times* Stanley Cup front page features an iPhone photograph taken after the newspaper's professional photojournalists were laid off.

ics and displays only a small, rather unengaging iPhone photo of the team captain carrying the Stanley Cup centered within a large red background. Taking up only about 13 percent of the layout, this photo is small because it lacks sharp enough focus for enlargement without degrading the image considerably. Despite an enormous headline that declares "Cup of Cheer," the photo itself does not appear either cheerful or celebratory. The team captain carrying the cup is not smiling, and there is no moment of jubilation frozen in time, as can be seen in the *Chicago Tribune*'s front page from the same date.

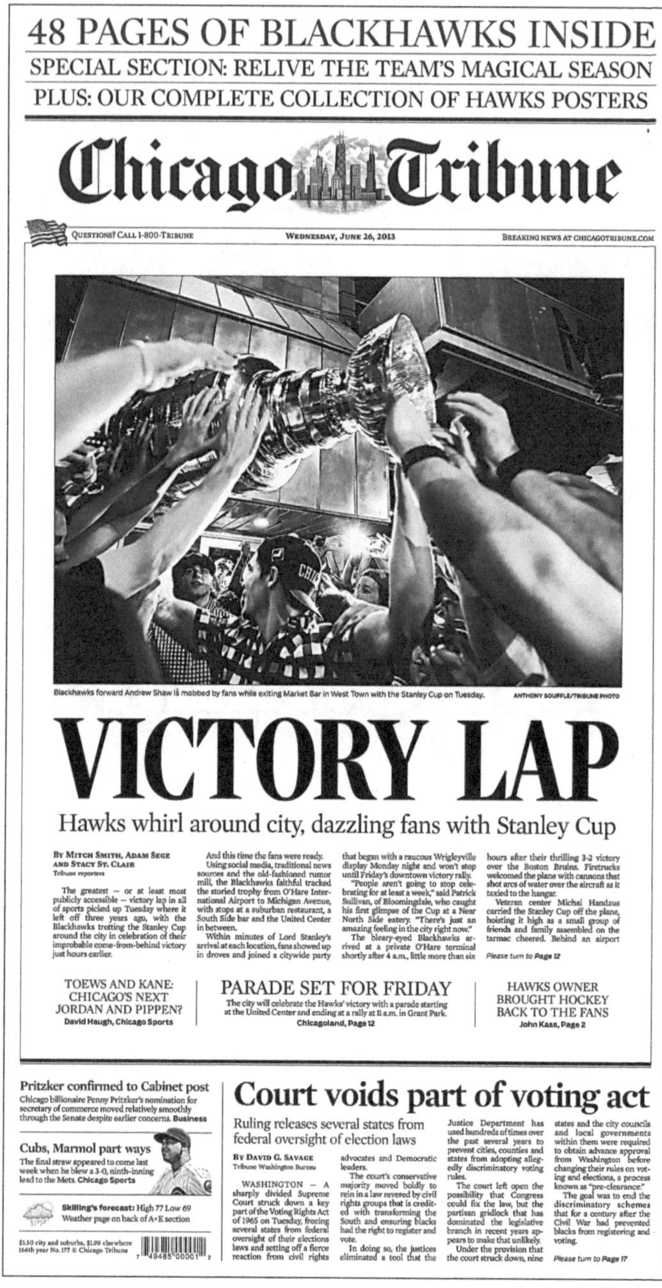

48 PAGES OF BLACKHAWKS INSIDE

SPECIAL SECTION: RELIVE THE TEAM'S MAGICAL SEASON

PLUS: OUR COMPLETE COLLECTION OF HAWKS POSTERS

Chicago Tribune

QUESTIONS? CALL 1-800-TRIBUNE | WEDNESDAY, JUNE 26, 2013 | BREAKING NEWS AT CHICAGOTRIBUNE.COM

Blackhawks forward Andrew Shaw is mobbed by fans while exiting Market Bar in West Town with the Stanley Cup on Tuesday. ANTHONY SOUFFLE/TRIBUNE PHOTO

VICTORY LAP

Hawks whirl around city, dazzling fans with Stanley Cup

BY MITCH SMITH, ADAM SEGE AND STACY ST. CLAIR
Tribune reporters

The greatest — or at least most publicly accessible — victory lap in all of sports picked up Tuesday where it left off three years ago, with the Blackhawks trotting the Stanley Cup around the city in celebration of their improbable come-from-behind victory just hours earlier.

And this time the fans were ready.

Using social media, traditional news sources and the old-fashioned rumor mill, the Blackhawks faithful tracked the storied trophy from O'Hare International Airport to Michigan Avenue, with stops at a suburban restaurant, a South Side bar and the United Center in between.

Within minutes of Lord Stanley's arrival at each location, fans showed up in droves and joined a citywide party that began with a raucous Wrigleyville display Monday night and won't stop until Friday's downtown victory rally.

"People aren't going to stop celebrating for at least a week," said Patrick Sullivan, of Bloomingdale, who caught his first glimpse of the Cup at a Near North Side eatery. "There's just an amazing feeling in the city right now."

The bleary-eyed Blackhawks arrived at a private O'Hare terminal shortly after 4 a.m., little more than six hours after their thrilling 3-2 victory over the Boston Bruins. Firetrucks welcomed the plane with cannons that shot arcs of water over the aircraft as it taxied to the hangar.

Veteran center Michal Handzus carried the Stanley Cup off the plane, hoisting it high as a small group of friends and family assembled on the tarmac cheered. Behind an airport

Please turn to Page 12

TOEWS AND KANE: CHICAGO'S NEXT JORDAN AND PIPPEN?
David Haugh, Chicago Sports

PARADE SET FOR FRIDAY
The city will celebrate the Hawks' victory with a parade starting at the United Center and ending at a rally at 11 a.m. in Grant Park.
Chicagoland, Page 12

HAWKS OWNER BROUGHT HOCKEY BACK TO THE FANS
John Kass, Page 2

Pritzker confirmed to Cabinet post
Chicago billionaire Penny Pritzker's nomination for secretary of commerce moved relatively smoothly through the Senate despite earlier concerns. **Business**

Cubs, Marmol part ways
The final straw appeared to come last week when he blew a 3-0, ninth-inning lead to the Mets. **Chicago Sports**

Skilling's forecast: High 77 Low 69
Weather page on back of A+E section

$1.50 city and suburbs, $1.99 elsewhere
166th year No. 177 © Chicago Tribune

Court voids part of voting act

Ruling releases several states from federal oversight of election laws

BY DAVID G. SAVAGE
Tribune Washington Bureau

WASHINGTON — A sharply divided Supreme Court struck down a key part of the Voting Rights Act of 1965 on Tuesday, freeing several states from federal oversight of their elections laws and setting off a fierce reaction from civil rights advocates and Democratic leaders.

The court's conservative majority moved boldly to rein in a law revered by civil rights groups that is credited with transforming the South and ensuring blacks had the right to register and vote.

In doing so, the justices eliminated a tool that the Justice Department has used hundreds of times over the past several years to prevent cities, counties and states from adopting allegedly discriminatory voting rules.

The court left open the possibility that Congress could fix the law, but the partisan gridlock that has dominated the legislative branch in recent years appears to make that unlikely.

Under the provision that the court struck down, nine states and the city councils and local governments within them were required to obtain advance approval from Washington before changing their rules on voting and elections, a process known as "pre-clearance."

The goal was to end the discriminatory schemes that for a century after the Civil War had prevented blacks from registering and voting.

Please turn to Page 17

This *Chicago Tribune* Stanley Cup front page features a photojournalist's shot of fans mobbing Blackhawks forward Andrew Shaw as he holds up the Stanley Cup. (Photo credit: 2013/Anthony Souffle/Chicago Tribune/TNS.)

In contrast, the *Tribune* photo, taken by a professional with professional equipment, could be enlarged enough to dominate the upper third of the page. This photo of a player with the cup being mobbed as he left a local bar actually *shows* celebration. Taken from the midst of a crowd with arms providing sight lines to the cup, it draws the viewer into the story rather than merely providing an illustration to accompany an oversized headline.

Professional Equipment

While cell-phone companies regularly boast increasing megapixels to improve image resolution and low-light capabilities, professional equipment also continues to improve. In addition, for sports photography and close-up work, telephoto and macro lenses are necessities that require major investments. For example, a 300mm lens typically used for sports can cost upward of $2,000 (Langton 2008; Kobre 2004; Horton 2001). It is nearly impossible to freeze action and detail the expressions of athletes in sporting events using an iPhone. In 2014 *St. Paul Pioneer Press* photojournalist Ben Garvin posted an April Fools' Day

Pioneer Press photojournalist Ben Garvin's 2014 April Fools' blog, which declared that the newspaper was shooting exclusively with iPhones, included this photo of Garvin shooting a Minnesota Timberwolves game next to photojournalists using telephoto lenses. (Photo by David Sherman.)

blog entitled "*Pioneer Press* photo staff to shoot exclusively with iPhones—April Fools!" (Garvin 2014). The blog spoofed the use of iPhones by newspapers and included a photograph of Garvin shooting a professional basketball game using an iPhone while sitting next to photojournalists using telephoto lenses on professional cameras.

Gehrz, winner of the 2014 National Press Photographers New America Award, said he occasionally uses an iPhone to get an image online quickly but more often than not relies on his professional equipment (Gehrz interview, March 25, 2013). For example, he described a situation in which some shooting suspects were at large. During the manhunt, a person was shot in the middle of the street. Because of the danger, Gehrz had to position himself at a safe distance, but was able to use a 300mm lens to get a detailed shot of the scene. Next to him was a reporter from the St. Paul newspaper, using an iPhone. Gehrz said that although he could not transmit his images back to the *Minneapolis Star Tribune* newsroom as quickly as the St. Paul reporter-photographer, his images had "much more impact" than those shot with an iPhone (Gehrz interview, March 25, 2013).

Reporters and Citizens as Photojournalists

In an article on how the *Chicago Sun-Times* is faring without a photo staff, Aja Romano (2013) describes a Tumblr page established to compare the newspaper to its rival, the *Chicago Tribune,* which still retains its photo staff. The article included a photo of a reporter holding a sign that states: "I'm a reporter. My photos suck!" According to Romano, the Tumblr page is "a visual illustration of what the former [*Sun-Times*] has lost along with its professional photography staff." In addition, she writes that, compared to the *Tribune*'s images, the *Sun-Times*'s photographs not only were bland, too far away from their subjects, and fewer in number but also lacked the vision that distinguishes professionals from amateurs. "It's that a true photographer knows when to snap a picture, and more importantly, what *kind* of picture equals a thousand words" (Romano 2013).

The management's layoff rationale at the *Sun-Times* (and also that of some managers at other metro dailies) that iPhones and amateur photography can replace professional photojournalism is based on the assumption that training, experience, and high-quality imagery do not make a difference. As Gehrz wrote in a 2015 e-mail, "Now if editors feel that in order to save money, they must eliminate or marginalize professional photojournalism, in my view, that is short sighted. I realize it may save money in the short run, just as firing all of your copyeditors for example, but it will never make the newspaper better."

Notably, although the amateur disaster and crisis photos receive high media visibility, the daily routine of a photojournalist is not limited to crisis and disaster situations. It includes a variety of assignments, such as groundbreakings, crime coverage, government coverage, community events coverage, and portraiture (Langton 2008; Kobre 2004; Horton 2001). Photojournalist Lisa DeYoung explained that, at the *Cleveland Plain Dealer,* "mostly . . . we cover the daily stuff that actually affects the quality of life for everyday Clevelanders. Like, Obama was here yesterday, so I photographed him in downtown Cleveland" (DeYoung interview). Certainly, citizens could not be expected to cover assignments with restricted access, such as presidential visits, press conferences, and professional sporting events. Nor could their availability be ensured on short notice when so many have occupational and family obligations. Deb Pastner, director of photo/multimedia for the *Minneapolis Star Tribune,* commented on the work of professionals. "I do believe in professionals," she said. "Pros shoot better than Joe Schmo. Most people shoot crappy photos" (Pastner interview).

Photo Sharing and Photojournalism as Different Modes of Communication

Websites such as Flickr and Photobucket archive billions of images and are virtually unmoderated sites that allow the public to easily upload and share photographs (Pink 2011; Van House 2011). These sites have few restrictions on topics, thus allowing people to post mundane and nontimely images for self-expression, for interacting with friends and relatives, for a visual diary, or for documentary proof of eyewitness status (Pink 2011; Van House 2011; Pantti and Bakker 2009; Murray 2008; Buehner 2011; Cohen 2005; Becker 2004).

Scholars Mikko Villi and Matteo Stocchetti (2011) situate photo sharing and photo messaging as social practices within the area of interpersonal communication. Unlike news photography that is informational communication, photo messaging is rarely undertaken for purely informative reasons and is most often used to express affection or as a gesture in itself rather than a venue for merely transmitting specific information (Villi and Stocchetti 2011; Pink 2011). Recent research on Instagram by Elisa Serafinelli (2017) reinforces these findings that photo sharing is largely a practice to advance social relationships. She finds that commonly "photography is experienced as an element of social connections" (109). In addition, as Barbie Zelizer and several other scholars have pointed out, citizen photographs serve as a verification of eye witnessing for friends and relatives rather than as a way of telling a story to the general public (Zelizer 2007; Allan 2013; Andén-Papadopoulos and Pantti 2011; Villi and Stocchetti 2011; Murray 2008; Cohen 2005).

While sharing photographs online has become increasingly popular, this interest does not mean that amateurs are engaged in all genres of photography, especially photojournalism. While citizen journalism and converging technologies have led to a blurring of the lines between professional photojournalists and amateurs, there are stylistic differences between amateur photography and professional photojournalists that do not make these images interchangeable. As noted in scholarship by Sarah Pink, Kris R. Cohen, Mikko Villi and Mateo Stocchetti, and Karin Becker, photoblogging and photo sharing are mostly done for social and expressive reasons and typically utilize a snapshot style described as almost an accidental, intuitive, casual style in which spontaneity is valued (Pink 2011; Villi and Stocchetti 2011; Cohen 2005; Becker 2004). This style often includes soft focus, under- or overexposure, or compositions that do not emphasize a dominant area or action area. The snapshot style contrasts with professional standards that include sharp focus, a range of detail in exposures, and framing for the dominant or action area (Kobre 2004; Horton 2001). In addition, newspapers typically expect professionals to be witnesses who are detached from their subjects, while nothing prevents citizens from involvement with the subjects they cover. This is problematic because detachment is critical to journalistic credibility, and it is why professional journalists working for news organizations are typically banned from involvement in political or social organizations. Even the appearance of a conflict of interest is perceived to jeopardize their credibility (Horton 2001). An additional problem with amateur images is that often the time, the day, or even the place in which they were taken cannot be verified (Pantti and Bakker 2009; Allan and Thorsen 2009; Becker 2004). These are the major reasons most of the metro dailies studied for this book do not regularly publish citizen photojournalism but rely on freelancers when staff photographers are unavailable (*Buffalo News* interviews; *Minneapolis Star Tribune* interviews, 2015–2019).

Professional Photojournalism and Storytelling

A professional photograph from the 2011 Occupy Minneapolis Movement depicts the storytelling demands required of a professional photojournalist. The Occupy Movement was started in New York in 2011 when demonstrators blocked Wall Street to protest economic and social injustice. With more than twenty years of experience as a photojournalist, *Star Tribune* photojournalist Jim Gehrz covered Occupy Minneapolis the year he was named Minnesota Photographer of the Year. Unlike the spontaneous, informal composition typical of the snapshot style, his photograph of an Occupy Minneapolis demonstration reflects the "decisive moment" approach introduced by photographer Henri Cartier-Bresson in the 1950s. This approach requires that the photographer observe a scene and wait until all the elements come together in the most engaging composition before taking the photograph (Cartier-Bresson 1952).

Star Tribune photojournalist Jim Gehrz shot this 2011 photo, which tells the story of an Occupy Minnesota demonstration that featured a meditating monk surrounded by noisy protestors. (Photo by Jim Gehrz. With permission from the *Minneapolis Star Tribune*.)

Gehrz's image tells the story of the demonstrations, depicting their diverse elements and capturing the mood or the essence of the event in a single shot. Here he has included a variety of people in various states of activity. Some are holding signs and shouting, some are taking photos, and some sit calmly in the foreground in peaceful protest. Gehrz described this image as "quiet in the midst of a storm" (Gehrz interview, March 25, 2013). While amateur news images can also reflect an eyewitness perspective, rarely are they intended to tell a story visually, as in this case.

Issues of Quality

The notion that iPhone photography by untrained writers or nonprofessionals can replace professional photojournalists, regardless of the lower quality of both the technical aspects and aesthetics, rests on a false assumption that professional standards, training, and experience are irrelevant (Irby 2002). While there are studies that attribute "authenticity" to blurry, poorly exposed, and poorly composed amateur images, it is doubtful that the high-quality, high-resolution standard of professional photography will be abandoned at a time when high-definition devices and Retinal Displays on iPads favor it (Mortensen 2014; Murray 2008; Dolan interviews, November 1, 2014, and February 15, 2016; Chan interview). Reinforcing this position are eye-track studies, which analyze eye movements to understand what attracts readers on page layouts and web pages. A number of these studies have been conducted since the beginning of the twenty-first century and have shown that visuals are powerfully engaging to readers both online and in print (S. Quinn 2007; Walker 2012; Nielsen Norman Group 2010).

In 2014 Poynter Institute researcher Sara Quinn conducted an eye-tracking study commissioned by the National Press Photographers Association that highlights the preference readers have for professional photographs compared to those submitted to newspapers by nonprofessionals. Countering the common layoff rationale that reporters with iPhones and nonprofessionals are adequate replacements for professionals, this study indicates readers were most attracted to high-quality professional images, and they found professional photography to be more memorable and more trustworthy than amateur images (S. Quinn 2015). According to Quinn, "Professional photographs were twice as likely as user-generated photographs to be shared" (S. Quinn 2015). People in the study also looked longer at professional photographs, and rated them highest among the photographs that they viewed. Also, Quinn said, "the importance of 'storytelling' to photography was mentioned by nearly every subject in the exit interviews" (S. Quinn 2015).

Given the results of the eye-tracking studies showing the attraction to professional images, Mark Dolan, former president of the National Press Photographers Association, admitted he was baffled by the layoff rationale that professionals are dispensable. At those newspapers, he said, "the bottom line is more important than quality" (Dolan interview, November 1, 2014).

Nonetheless, Dolan said he still believed "professional photojournalism will always be important" regardless of the platform on which it is presented (Dolan interview, February 15, 2016).

New Directions for Photojournalists

As newspaper staff positions in photojournalism have been cut, some laid-off photojournalists have freelanced or have taken positions in advertising, public relations, and education. Several photojournalists interviewed stated they believe photojournalism will persist whatever the platform, print or online (Chan interview; Curtiss interview; Denney interview; DeYoung interview; Dolan interviews; Gehrz interviews; Kordalski interview; Lambert interview; Pastner interview; Peterson interview; Pinkley interview; Rendleman interviews; Strasburg interview). Michelle LaVigne, formerly of the *Chicago Sun-Times,* now has her own photography business, Photomoxie Studios (LaVigne interview). Her work involves portraits, events, weddings, and full documentation of families. She said she enjoys this work and feels she is basically using the same skills she used as a photojournalist.

Some former newspaper photojournalists are also joining photographic collectives and co-ops such as Magnum and Contact Press Images. Luceo is a New York–based photographic cooperative formed in 2007 in which members share the responsibilities for marketing and distribution (Estrin 2010). Luceo members also set aside a portion of their commercial and editorial commissions for a fund to support long-term member projects. In his 2013 book, *Bending the Frame,* Fred Ritchin writes about photo collectives in some countries that work on long-term documentary projects, or "Slow Journalism." In addition, the trend in entrepreneurial journalism has opened up positions and assignments for photojournalists as new news sites emerge.

Ritchin also highlights new directions for photojournalism outside of the newspaper industry. "As editorial publications suffer from reduced funding and limit their coverage of the news, humanitarian organizations have taken a larger role in documenting hot spots, combined with advocacy" (2013, 18). Ritchin writes that, in their work with humanitarian organizations, photojournalists are able to take a hybrid approach to their work between the first-person perspective of the citizen journalist and the third-person perspective of the journalist. In addition, he states that this reinvention of photojournalism could overcome some of the sensationalistic and formulaic uses of photojournalism so common in mainstream media outlets.

Conclusion

Although newspaper photojournalism has suffered severe cutbacks in the twenty-first century, this does not mean that photojournalism is a dying field. Within the context of the declining newspaper industry shifting to multiplatform delivery, newspapers have also lost considerable numbers of writers, editors, and other staff members. The disparity between cutbacks of photojournalists and other staff members can be attributed to their inferior status and the high cost of photo departments. While a common refrain for eliminating photojournalists has been that reporters with iPhones and citizen photojournalists are adequate replacements, these short-term solutions are based on the false assumption that quality, training, and experience are irrelevant. Quinn's eye-tracking study, as well as studies conducted previously, indicates that the general public prefers higher-quality, high-resolution professional photography and that they are apt to remember specific professional images as well as share them with others.

Until the newspaper industry is able to reverse its decline, there will continue to be layoffs throughout the industry, and there will continue to be a need for research on where the industry is headed and the effects on visual journalists. For those photojournalists who are laid off, this is not the end of the road. Some are freelancing, some are working with online news sites, and some are working with nonprofit humanitarian organizations (Kirkland 2014; LaVigne interview). Those who remain at metro dailies continue to work under the pressure of periodic layoffs, increased workloads, and 24/7 Internet deadlines, yet most of the photojournalists interviewed for this book expressed both a passion for and a dedication to their work. Despite the current challenges to the profession, Gus Chan, a photojournalist at the *Cleveland Plain Dealer,* said he remains optimistic about photojournalism in the future: “Photographers are a thoughtful lot, and they *will* persevere” (Chan interview).

3

The *Cleveland Plain Dealer*

Digital First and a Newsroom Divided

Note: Fear of company retaliation for some of the comments made by Plain Dealer *staff members in this chapter necessitated the speakers' anonymity. In addition, the management at the Northeast Ohio Media Group (now called Advance Ohio) denied permission for staff members to be interviewed for this book, and severance pay packages for laid-off staffers were contingent on their refraining from making disparaging public remarks about the company. Vice President of Content Chris Quinn e-mailed me on September 14, 2015, denying my request for interviews: "We are a bit sensitive here about interviews such as this because we've seen a fair share of writers of bad will with agendas. They have not written about us accurately or fairly, and we have concluded that the best course of action is to ignore them. They don't have large audiences, and by not responding, we don't add gasoline to the fires they try to build." Despite the complications that resulted from the media group's refusal to participate in the research for this book, I was able to provide context for Advance's Digital-First motivations and the implementation of Digital-First strategies through both industry and scholarly literature and interviews with* Plain Dealer *staff members.*

On the evening of July 30, 2013, staff members at the *Cleveland Plain Dealer* received an e-mail telling them to stay home the following morning between the hours of 8:00 A.M. and 10:00 A.M. to wait for a phone call about whether or not they still had a job. Although the layoffs of approximately fifty, or one-third of the newsroom, had been announced months earlier, the final word would come down to a phone call over a two-hour period—a waiting period one reporter described in a *Columbia Journalism Review* article as "slow torture" (Clark 2013). Wendy McManamon, an award-winning copyeditor and the chair of the *Plain Dealer*'s unit of the Northeast Ohio Newspaper Guild, described this time as "nerve-wracking" (McManamon interview, March 17, 2016).

According to David Kordalski, the *Plain Dealer*'s assistant managing editor for visuals who retired in 2016, from the perspective of management, layoffs are difficult for the news organizations as well. Although Kordalski knew his job was safe, he had been involved in the layoff evaluations of the people he supervised, even though he did not make the final decisions. Because a number of people volunteered for buyouts, that took "some of the sting out of it" (Kordalski interview, March 20, 2016). Nonetheless it was difficult for him because he was responsible for making calls to those staff members who were retained but who did not know the nature of the call. Consequently, as they initially answered the phone, things "were pretty frosty" (Kordalski interview, March 20, 2016). "There's no good way to do layoffs," he added. "I hear horror stories about people in newsrooms who get called into the office individually and their last act in the office is having a tantrum or breaking down and crying or trying to be stoic while they're being told and carrying their belongings out. There's just no good way to do layoffs."

Save the *Plain Dealer* Campaign

In 2012, even before the mass layoffs and the division of the newsrooms into three separate locations, the newspaper guild initiated an online petition to alert readers to some of the changes that the *Plain Dealer*'s parent corporation, Advance Publications, was planning. Its Save the *Plain Dealer* campaign was launched when Advance announced plans to reduce delivery days to three or four days a week, sparking fears that publication days would also be reduced as they had been at other Advance newspapers, especially the *New Orleans Times-Picayune* (Theim 2013c; Edmonds 2014a). Although it was unclear what would be done in Cleveland, the guild created a multimedia campaign to inform the public of the pattern of reorganization common to Advance newspapers, which included reversing priorities from print to the Web, along with cutbacks in delivery and/or publication days as well as "massive" layoffs of staff members (Edmonds 2014a). Although this campaign did not prevent layoffs or the reduction of home delivery days, the company's agreement to continue the seven-day-a-week publication and reduce only the newspaper's home-delivery days was considered somewhat of a victory (Theim 2013c).

"Goodbye Cleveland"

In a photo that was circulated online, a number of staff members commemorated the layoffs by posing for a family photograph of sorts in front of the *Plain Dealer* building, holding signs that said "Goodbye Cleveland" and "PD Cuts Hurt NE Ohio" and one lamenting Cleveland's loss of a "great newspaper" (Beaujon et al. 2014). While a reduction in staff did not literally mean the end of the *Plain Dealer*, it did mark the end of its newsroom culture. This culture was described by various staff members as collegial, informal, collaborative, and reflective of the pride in building the *Plain Dealer*'s national reputation as a top-ranking metro daily known for quality journalism, especially investigative journalism. McManamon noted that, when the staff returned to the newsroom, "it was like a bomb had gone off in the building. This big, spacious lively newsroom was just hushed and it was like we had all been uprooted" (McManamon interview, March 17, 2016).

The layoffs also marked the beginning of a new digitally oriented newsroom culture imposed by Advance Publications, which was prescribed for all of its newspaper holdings. This new newsroom culture displaced the communal culture that had developed at the *Plain Dealer* over decades. Emphasizing a "Digital-First" approach, this culture reversed the traditional priority given to print and required journalists to make several online postings daily while working on an assignment or shortly after completing one. It also stressed individual competition as measured in online analytics or metrics (the number of clicks individual stories received) and an emphasis on backpack journalism that requires reporters to do writing, video, and still photography from the field. In addition, the company required newsroom workspaces to be depersonalized to allow for multiple users (*Plain Dealer* interviews, 2015).

Since 2013, additional rounds of layoffs have reduced the newspaper staff to approximately 39 from a peak of approximately 350 in 2000 (McManamon e-mail; Clark 2014c; Sterne 2013). Accompanying the layoffs were cost-cutting measures involving reducing home delivery from seven days per week to four, with non-delivery-day newspapers available only at newsstands. One of the most drastic changes in 2013 was the reorientation requiring the *Plain Dealer* staff to adopt a "Digital-First" approach in which cleveland.com was given priority over the *Plain Dealer.*

These changes were instituted in just a few months—the company announced them in April and implemented them in August (Miller 2014; Fladung interview). Digital First contrasts with the multiplatform approach utilized by many U.S. and European newspapers in which content is distributed to print and online without prioritizing a platform, or a modified Digital-First approach in which breaking news is a priority for desktop and mobile platforms, while print is still considered a key platform (Carvajal and Aviles 2008; Aviles and Carvajal 2008; Doyle 2013, 2015; Lischka 2015; Bressers 2006).

The company's aggressive Digital-First approach also emphasized the immediacy of the news by requiring "iterative reporting," or short online postings soon after an assignment is undertaken and before the story is fully sourced and written. In other words, the story is posted in chunks that are expected to be updated frequently as the story is written for publication in the newspaper. This contrasts with the journalistic practice of completing a story and fully vetting its sources before publication. Scholarly studies of journalistic practices have emphasized the loss of quality standards when speed in posting new content in this style takes precedence over traditional journalistic values of accuracy and balance (Phillips 2014; Ryfe 2012; Lee-Wright, Phillips, and Witschge 2011).

To reinforce its backpack journalism initiative, Advance gave reporters and editors laptops, iPhones, and backpacks to facilitate working from home or from a café or coffee shop. According to an anonymous reporter quoted in a 2014 *Columbia Journalism Review* article, "They are very much encouraging us to be mobile, to not claim particular places [in the newsroom] and not keep a lot of stuff there" (Clark 2014c).

Additional Digital-First Transformations

Certainly the *Cleveland Plain Dealer* is not unique because of its staff reductions. Layoffs and buyouts have affected metropolitan dailies across the United States for several years. What *is* unique about this newspaper's situation is its divided newsrooms. Rather than having a single news staff working together on both print and online products, it has separate facilities for its nonunion Advance Ohio staff and its unionized *Plain Dealer* staff. In conjunction with the 2013 layoffs, Advance established a separate nonunion company called the Northeast Ohio Media Group (now Advance Ohio) that was responsible for cleveland.com. Although the new company was located in a separate facility from that of the *Plain Dealer,* both staffs were expected to contribute to both the website and the newspaper.

In addition, the *Plain Dealer* staff was split into two separate newsrooms in separate facilities: one for its content producers (reporters and editors) and one for its production staff (copyeditors and designers). Initially each group was moved to a smaller space in the *Plain Dealer* building as it was renovated to accommodate the website staff. Eventually the *Plain Dealer* content producers moved to a smaller leased space in an office tower more than a mile away that is about one-fourth the size of their former newsroom. Meanwhile, their colleagues, the production staff, were moved to a third location several miles away called the "Pub Hub."

This chapter examines Advance Publications' solution to the challenge of making online news profitable by using a one-size-fits-all Digital-First model for its daily newspapers and its rapid implementation of this policy in Cleveland (Miller 2014; Clark 2013). This policy was first implemented at a large metro daily in 2012, when Advance reduced publication of the *New Orleans Times-Picayune* to three days a week both to cut costs and to drive readers to the Web version of the newspaper. Accompanying this "digital pivot" were substantial layoffs and the requirement that journalists make online a priority through frequent postings and an emphasis on producing popular stories that would get clicks (Theim 2013a). While Advance claimed that its strategy would pay off in Cleveland by 2015 and that online readership was increasing rapidly, the company has been criticized for its rigid and rapid implementation of what former *Times-Picayune* reporter Rebecca Theim described as its "draconian digital-first business strategy" (Edmonds 2015; Theim 2013c). And while some critics agreed with Advance that the future of journalism is online, they also expressed concern that Advance's Digital-First approach was very "premature" (Miller 2014; McManamon interview, September 29, 2015). I focus here on the transition from prioritizing print to an aggressively digital strategy that has changed not only newsroom practices and work routines but also the overall newsroom culture at the *Plain Dealer* and the lives of the individuals on its staff.

Economics of Digital and Print Platforms

In 2019 Cleveland's population was about 390,000, down from a population of 1 million that peaked in 1950 before the decline of the steel industry. The *Plain Dealer* has been the only metro daily in the city since the 1980s, and, like other metro dailies, it relies on print advertising for the bulk of its revenue. Consequently, its profits are directly tied to the ability of Cleveland's business sector to purchase advertising. As a result of the recession that started at the end of 2007, advertising revenue fell precipitously. Although I was not given access to the website staff for financial information on cleveland.com, 2014 statistics were published in *Crain's Cleveland Business* (Miller 2014). According to the media group's former president, Andrea Hogben, cleveland.com typically drew 6 to 7 million unique visitors per month who viewed 50 million pages, and this compared to 4 million copies of the print newspaper sold each month. The Pew Research Center's statistics for January 2015 confirm these statistics: cleveland.com had 6.497 million unique viewers that month (Barthel 2015b). It should be noted that the author of the *Crain's* article, Jay Miller, cautioned against directly comparing online page views to the numbers of newspapers sold each month because people read differently online and in print. Typically print readers are more thorough readers of the newspaper, while online readers graze the news, rarely reading it page by page (Miller 2014). In 2016 the *Plain Dealer*'s circulation figures were 200,702 for daily circulation, down from a prerecession figure in 2006 of 343,163, and its Sunday circulation was 264,834, down from 450,875 in 2006 (Alliance for Audited Media 2016).

Miller's story also pointed out that although "digital advertising is growing in dimes while advertising revenue is moving away from print in dollars," Hogben considered cleveland.com profitable because in 2014 it brought in 20 percent of Advance's advertising revenue and this was higher than the national average of approximately 13 percent (Miller 2014). Significantly, this also means that 80 percent of its advertising revenue still came from the *Plain Dealer,* despite the fact that it was home-delivered only four days a week.

Advance's Digital-First Strategies

During some of the interviews for this book staff members expressed concern that Advance did not seem to have clear-cut strategies for implementing their digital pivot, as evident in the coverage overlaps between the print and online staffs, changes in daily quotas for posting several stories and multimedia packages, and changes in home delivery days from three to four days after advertisers objected (interviews, 2015–2018). However, some media analysts and scholars have identified the influence of media consultant Clayton Christiansen in Advance's strategies (Chyi 2013; Edmonds 2014b). Advance adopted his advice almost purely on the basis of a disruptive innovation theory that envisions an all-digital future: It separated its print and online operations, it invested in its online operations, and it divested from its print operations (Doctor 2013a; Edmonds 2014a, 2014b). Ken Doctor (2013a), Harvard University's Nieman Lab media analyst, examined the Digital-First model Advance implemented at the *Oregonian*, the *New Orleans Times-Picayune*, and the *Plain Dealer.* His assessment of Advance's Digital-First strategies emphasizes their costs:

> Stand back from this audacious strategy—with all its staff-cutting pain, its inducing of reader pain, and the promise of its digital-first, future-is-now thinking—and it's hard to get past the point of its missing digital reader revenue strategy. . . . When it came time to acknowledge basic truths about newspapering, Advance management reached for the hand grenade rather than the scalpel. . . . Reading the same tea leaves of print decline as their brethren, they decided that blowing up the enterprise (reassembling it in two pieces) and downsizing their operations, their home delivery, and their community service was the answer. (Doctor 2013a)

When unveiling the company's digital strategies, Terrance Egger, president, publisher, and chief executive of the *Plain Dealer,* explained that the reduced delivery days were established to meet the "evolving needs of our print and online audiences" (quoted in Trickey 2013). Egger also explained that Digital First was intended to drive consumers online and to engage young readers who use digital platforms (Miller 2013). However, *Cleve-*

land Magazine writer Erick Trickey noted that this rationale did not make sense in light of cleveland.com's poorly designed, template-based website, which was hardly user friendly, and its substandard online content, which did not "live up to the company's digital ambition" (Trickey 2013).

Although some critics claimed Advance's strategies were "unnecessary and premature" in light of the fact that print was still bringing in the bulk of the newspaper's revenue, Egger stated that an all-digital future was inevitable (Trickey 2013; Miller 2013). In terms of the economics of reduced home delivery days, media analyst Rick Edmonds expressed doubt that Advance's savings from reducing home delivery days would compensate for the inevitable losses in lucrative display advertising on nondelivery days (Edmonds 2014a, 2014b). Nonetheless, Advance was steadfast in implementing its Digital-First model, despite the fact that at the time of its implementation only about 34 percent of Cleveland's residents had the high-speed Internet capability that is necessary for accessing cleveland.com (Trickey 2013).

History of the *Plain Dealer*

The *Plain Dealer* was established as a weekly newspaper in 1842 and became an evening daily in 1845 (Case Western Reserve University 1997). In 1885 attorney and developer Liberty Holden bought the newspaper and added morning and Sunday editions. The evening edition was discontinued in 1905. Holden's heirs became owners of the newspaper in 1913 and remained in control of the newspaper until the late 1960s. In 1933, the *Plain Dealer* became the city's largest newspaper, and although it acquired its competitor, the *Cleveland News*, the two papers continued operating independently. In 1960 the *Cleveland News* was sold to the *Cleveland Press*, which eventually was shuttered in 1982, making the *Plain Dealer* the only major metropolitan newspaper in the city. In 1967 the *Plain Dealer* was sold to the S. I. Newhouse newspaper group, a private company, and it continues to be controlled by the Newhouse family under the umbrella of Advance Publications, Inc.

The *Plain Dealer* is known for having the largest circulation of any newspaper in the state of Ohio and has been ranked among the top twenty-five U.S. Sunday newspapers with digital editions (Barthel 2015b). The newspaper has received two Pulitzer Prizes as well as numerous Associated Press and statewide journalism awards.

Originally, cleveland.com was staffed by the *Plain Dealer*. This ended in 2013, when Advance Publications established the Northeast Ohio Media Group as a separate nonunion company responsible for operating the website. The media group, which changed its name to Advance Ohio in 2016, is responsible for all the advertising sales and marketing for the *Plain Dealer*, cleveland.com, and the *Sun Newspapers*, a group of small weekly suburban newspapers.

The Newhouse Job Security/Anti-union Pledge

Former *Times-Picayune* reporter Rebecca Theim has written about the Newhouse family pledge that once promised lifetime job security in exchange for keeping unions out of its newspaper holdings (2013c). This pledge was eventually rescinded "as the industry's 30-percent profit margins evaporated . . . and employees were let go in droves without so much as a shop steward's shoulder to cry on" (Theim 2013c).

Although the details of the creation of the pledge are sketchy, it is believed that Samuel Newhouse wrote it in the mid-1960s following labor unrest, strikes, and violence during negotiations that had emerged back in the 1930s at several of the company's newspapers (Theim 2013c). This promise was widely known in the newspaper industry and was considered a major factor in staving off unions at Advance newspapers because only two of its more than thirty dailies, the *Cleveland Plain Dealer* and the *Newark Star-Ledger*, are union shops. In 2009, however, as newspaper profits continued to decline, Advance rescinded its pledge. In her book about Advance that details the layoffs and the discontinuance of daily publication at the *New Orleans Times-Picayune*, Theim discusses mass layoffs in two states. She writes that Advance's terminations at the *Times-Picayune* and three newspapers in Alabama on a single day in 2012 "became responsible for close to one-third of all jobs eliminated in 2012 at the nation's almost 1,400 daily newspapers" (Theim 2013b, 74).

In 2013 the layoffs at the *Plain Dealer* that accompanied the "digital pivot" were implemented at several other Advance newspapers as well:

> [These layoffs] began in short order and on a staggering scale at company newspapers in Alabama, Michigan, Louisiana, New York, Ohio, Oregon, and Pennsylvania. By September 2013, "digital first" had claimed about 1,600 newspaper jobs from Portland, OR, to Mobile, AL. (Theim 2013c)

Studies indicate that these ongoing rounds of layoffs, also common at other metro dailies, result in persistent pressure on staff members that not only depletes their morale but also fosters a timid approach to reporting; reduced interest in investigative and public service reporting; and an inclination to report on commercially viable, entertainment-oriented stories to attract online readers (Phillips 2014; Ryfe 2012; Lee-Wright, Phillips, and Witschge 2011; Edge 2014a; Witschge and Nygren 2009).

Scott Reinardy's study of daily newspapers describes how industry-wide layoffs of veterans "decimated institutional and community knowledge creating a cultural gap of work routines and practices" (2016, x). His ethnographic work articulates the tremendous pressure on surviving staff members caught between "two journalistic worlds": one, the traditional news world of detachment and depersonalization, and the other, the personalized world of the Internet and social media. Reinardy's work details how assembly-line journalism, with its daily quotas for several online postings and the 24/7 multimedia demands of the Internet, has created an "unbearable and unfulfilling" pace at newspapers across the United States (20). This has led to not only less journalistic autonomy but also lowered quality standards, as content that attracts "web clicks and quick-hit journalism" takes precedence over "quality work based on good sourcing and editing" (Reinardy 2016, 20). Reinardy also highlights another loss to the industry as high-salaried veterans are laid off or bought out: Young journalists can no longer benefit from the mentorship roles veterans had assumed in the past to introduce new staff members to the newsroom culture.

Consequently, as several *Plain Dealer* staff members emphasized in interviews for this chapter, the fears of layoffs and the increased workloads with a bare bones staff generally resulted in lower standards of reporting and a devastated morale (*Plain Dealer* interviews, 2015–2019). There has been less time to do investigative and in-depth pieces, less time to do balanced sourcing, and less time to do thorough editing. These are concerns prominent in literature on newspapers as well as in other areas of media as staffs try to balance print and online/multimedia and social media responsibilities (Phillips 2014; Brüggemann et al. 2016; Ryfe 2012; Lee-Wright, Phillips, and Witschge 2011; Witschge and Nygren 2009; O'Sullivan and Heinonen 2008).

Newspaper Liquidation Theory

According to a *Columbia Journalism Review* article by Ryan Chittum, the newspaper layoffs and Advance's other Digital-First policies are part of its "newspaper liquidation plan," reflecting the company's anti-union stance as well as its emphasis on an all-digital future (2013a). Using a similar template for all of its newspaper holdings, this approach has left Advance newspapers with "gutted newsrooms, reduced publication and a turn to the hamster-wheel model of digital journalism." The "hamster-wheel model" Chittum refers to is the nonstop breaking news cycle required by online news. In terms of liquidation of its newspapers, Chittum explained that, during the recession, before the pledge was totally rescinded, Advance had amended the pledge to state that there would be no layoffs of regular employees "due to technological change or economic conditions, *as long as our newspaper continues to publish daily in its current newsprint form*" (Chittum 2013a, emphasis in original). Consequently, this

Wendy McManamon, award-winning copyeditor and newspaper guild chairwoman, has expressed concern about the downsizing of the *Plain Dealer*'s staff as a strategy for dismantling the newspaper's guild. (Photo by Doug Nemanic, 2015.)

indicated to Chittum that the newsprint format was slated for demise, opening the door for mass layoffs and eventually allowing the company to shift to digital-only without a union staff.

In the wake of the 2013 layoffs, Advance's staunch anti-union stance led to charges of union busting at the *Plain Dealer*. Some staff members and critics described splitting the newsroom into three separate locations and the establishment of the nonunion Northeast Ohio Media Group as a separate company as divide-and-conquer strategies to dismantle the newspaper guild (*Plain Dealer* interviews, 2015; Theim 2013a). In a *Columbia Journalism Review* article, McManamon described the situation: "It smells and looks like union busting. They will say this is how they do it in other markets, but in no other market do they have a union staff and a non-union staff" (quoted in Clark 2014a). Reinforcing this sentiment is the guild's concession to Advance that in its 2019 contract negotiations the *Plain Dealer* will no longer be a closed union shop, giving the company the option of hiring either union or nonunion employees. According to some critics, this gives the company virtually no incentive to hire union employees (Theim 2013a).

In addition, while staff members were told that moving the production staff to the company's property outside of the downtown area would amount to saving the high cost of leasing additional newsroom space in the prime downtown location of Tower City, some staff members said they believed this was more of a divide-and-conquer tactic to undercut the newsroom culture and diffuse the power of the newspaper guild (*Plain Dealer* interviews, 2015; Clark 2014a; Theim 2013c). As Theim points out, only two of more than thirty Advance newspapers are unionized, the *Plain Dealer* and the *Newark Star-Ledger*, and Advance's historically high salaries reflect its success in staving off unionization.

> In New Orleans, there was never any question about the relationship between The Pledge and Advance's anti-union position. Former and a few remaining *Times-Picayune* employees recall annual employee presentations by longtime Publisher Ashton Phelps, Jr. in which he usually ended with a declaration of the company's dislike of unions followed by a recitation of The Pledge. (2013c)

Other newspaper companies have also demonstrated a pattern of using periodic layoffs in an effort to not only cut costs but also diminish or eliminate newspaper unions or guilds. In 2013 Michigan newspaper unions warned of union busting by the Journal Register Company, whose chief executive officer was John Paton of Digital First Media (Beaujon 2013; Hamm 2013b). Paton is often quoted for his definition of the Digital-First approach as "Digital First, Print Last" (E. Sterling 2011). In a bulletin sent to union members at two Michigan newspapers, the guild reported that the company was utilizing the circumstances of bankruptcy as an excuse to lay off employees and then require them to reapply for their jobs at lower salaries with fewer benefits (Beaujon 2013). The union added that the company had a reputation for its union-busting strategies in markets such as Philadelphia and New York. In 2014, union members at the *Denver Post* and at *El Diario* in New York City held rallies demonstrating against the union-busting tactics of their newspapers' parent companies (Hutchins 2016; AFL-CIO New York City Central Labor Council 2014).

By the summer of 2013 approximately one-third of the *Plain Dealer* newsroom was gone, and the media group was being developed as a separate nonunion news company. A major source of tension then erupted between former colleagues as Advance raided the *Plain Dealer* to start the media group, giving select staff members twenty-four hours to accept higher-paying positions without union contracts and with fewer benefits (Clark 2014b). The media group also hired a number of less experienced reporters and multimedia producers while the staff of the *Plain Dealer* was told to expect more layoffs in 2014 (Sandy 2013).

Iterative Reporting: A New Style for Online News Work

Although Advance provided some training in new methods and software a few weeks before implementing its digital pivot, several staff members said they found the transition very difficult. Particularly challenging was the adaptation to prioritizing cleveland.com over the *Plain Dealer* as well as to adjusting to the online writing style of iterative reporting or posting online chunks of a story before it has been completely vetted and written. Former *Plain Dealer* managing editor Thom Fladung described this style of reporting as bringing about "the most profound change in the business and in my career" (Fladung interview). He added that in the past

> one of the most central ethics of daily newspapering was: you don't publish the story until you have the story. And having the story involved getting something from all the people involved in the story, or at least making a really hard run at it. And so we held stories. . . . Now—you can't

> hold stories. Now the ethic is: I'm going to do the story iteratively so you're involved in this story and two other people are involved in the story. And I talked to those people and I have all the facts and you didn't return my call—tough—the story's going, and maybe you'll return my call then and maybe I'll add you to my story or maybe I'll do a new story. (Fladung interview)

While iterative reporting was developed for a sense of immediacy and to situate the website as the place for breaking news, it has been criticized for its lack of balance and for the style's emphasis on rapid postings of a story before it is fully vetted and edited (Phillips 2014; Ryfe 2012; Lee-Wright, Phillips, and Witschge 2011). Staff members also noted that the spelling and grammatical errors that appeared in these raw posts were especially embarrassing when readers posted their corrections. Kordalski said of iterative reporting, "I hate it." As a reader who is "just trying to consume news[,] . . . I don't have an editor's time to put that [the whole story] together. . . . I'm just trying to get information, and when they don't wrap it up, I feel I've been cheated of information in my community that I need." Nonetheless, as a journalist, Kordalski said he understands why this style is popular because it makes an online news operation competitive. However, "the bottom line is that the people who are consuming your news, they don't care who's first, they care who's accurate and who gives them a complete picture" (Kordalski interview, March 20, 2016).

A particularly controversial example of the problems precipitated by iterative reporting involved cleveland.com's coverage of the death of Tamir Rice in 2014. Rice was a twelve-year-old black child with a toy pellet gun who was killed by Cleveland police. Initial coverage of the death on cleveland.com was criticized for emphasizing the violent domestic background of Rice's parents, which critics described as implying they were somehow responsible for his death. This coverage was generally criticized for its lack of context in profiling the case and for its neglect of reporting on the background of the police officers involved. The media group responded to criticism with this justification: "People from across the region have been asking whether Rice grew up around violence. The Northeast Ohio Media Group investigated the backgrounds of the parents and found the mother and father both have violent pasts" (Clark 2014d). In response to "public backlash" by the newspaper staff and audience members, a *Columbia Journalism Review* article noted that a cleveland.com column by Reader Representative Ted Diadiun acknowledged this criticism. But, according to Anna Clark, he "then brushed concerns aside: 'This is an imperfect process, and will remain so. But news at the speed of light is here to stay, and we are all going to have to get used to it'" (Clark 2014d).

Some critics rejected cleveland.com's justification for its coverage and expressed concern that, instead of developing a full profile of the case, which could have included details on Rice's family history, the website presented the history of violence out of context. McManamon was quoted in the article: "Call me old-school, but if this particular story were presented to a newspaper editor of any integrity, they likely would reject it as incomplete. . . . Can you imagine Ben Bradlee reading such a one-sided report and saying, 'Post it right away'?" (Clark 2014d). A Facebook posting by Kordalski was also quoted in the article: "If I have anything to do with it, this will not appear in the print editions of *The Plain Dealer*" (Clark 2014d).

The *Columbia Journalism Review* also criticized the website's use of iterative reporting, saying that on

> a story as fraught and combustible as the Tamir Rice shooting—involving police violence, racial tensions, the death of a child, and public anger, unfolding while protests are still ongoing in Ferguson, MO—iterative reporting is an accident waiting to happen. Bits-and-pieces coverage has the ring of hasty gossip. Even if the posts do accumulate into a solid narrative, many readers will glean only a portion of it—catching pieces as they stream on Cleveland.com, or on Facebook, and missing the whole. (Clark 2014d)

The article also noted the tension that had arisen between the website staff and the newspaper staff because readers did not know that the website and the newspaper were separate companies with separate staffs. McManamon was quoted as saying:

> Readers will see posts on *cleveland.com* and don't distinguish between reporters of NEOMG [the media group] and *The Plain Dealer,* so when there is something as shameful as this Tamir Rice tidbit, the public lashes out at *The Plain Dealer.* (Clark 2014d)

McManamon noted that the emphasis on posting iterative reports as quickly as possible had also lowered the standards for the website because many of these stories are uploaded with little or no editing by news editors or the copy desk. This was evident in April 2016 when cleveland.com posted a story about a threat that the National Basketball Association would pull the all-star game out of North Carolina unless the state repealed the sexist "bathroom law"—a story that had only one source: a hoax website made to look like the ABC News site (Bucholtz 2016). Vice President of Content Chris Quinn publicly apologized because the story was posted without source verification. "We should have found other sources, and, finding none, questioned how ABC would be alone in reporting this story. If we had done the basics, we would have figured out pretty quickly that we were seeing an impostor ABC website" (C. Quinn 2016). Quinn also apologized for attributing some of the information to the Associated Press:

> Our second mistake was in how we reported the fake news. We combined it with an Associated Press story about the North Carolina controversy but left the AP byline on what we published. That made it appear that the Associated Press had been duped by the impostor website. That's not fair to the Associated Press, a valued partner for *cleveland.com.* (C. Quinn 2016)

The Fragmentation of the Newsroom

While the former *Plain Dealer* newsroom (in a building owned by Advance) was being remodeled for the website staff, the *Plain Dealer* reporters and editors were temporarily relocated to an unoccupied conference-sized room just outside the main newsroom that one staff member estimated was approximately twelve feet by twelve feet. Copyeditors and the graphics staff, also formerly in the main newsroom, were located in another small room three floors above the reporters and editors. Several staff members said these spaces reinforced their feelings of being devalued by the company and added to the demoralization they already felt from the digital pivot (*Plain Dealer* interviews, 2015–2019). Eventually reporters and editors were moved to a permanent location more than a mile away that was about one-fourth of the size of their former newsroom, while the copyeditors and graphics staff were moved to the printing plant about one-half hour away. One area of concern about the *Plain Dealer*'s future is the fact that the lease for the downtown newsroom expired in 2019 at the same time as the guild contract did, triggering fears that Advance will eliminate the *Plain Dealer altogether* and move to a digital-only format as they have done at some of their newspapers—providing further support for the newspaper liquidation theory detailed by Chittum (Clark 2014a; Chittum 2013a).

During the remodeling of the *Plain Dealer*'s former newsroom to accommodate the staff, a photo of its dismantling was posted online with the caption, "This used to be a newsroom" (Clark 2014c). It symbolized not only the fragmentation of the newsroom but also the sense, according to many of the remaining *Plain Dealer* staff members, that "the newsroom culture is gone." In interviews, several staff members said they missed the interaction they had with their colleagues (*Plain Dealer* interviews, 2015–2018). Before the 2013 layoffs, Kordalski said the *Plain Dealer* had developed into an award-winning newspaper with a bustling newsroom where people talked back and forth and shared information. At that time the newspaper was consistently winning awards for excellence, including a Pulitzer Prize "that was a huge momentum boost for us" (Kordalski interviews, March 20, 2016 and September 29, 2015). Then "all of a sudden, things abruptly changed. . . . [T]hat was tough" (Kordalski interview, March 20, 2016). One reporter quoted in a *Columbia Journalism Review* article described the change in newsroom culture in 2013: "There's not a newsroom buzz. There's not camaraderie of the newsroom, where everyone is hearing what's going on. You're off doing your separate thing" (Clark 2014c). Another staff member missed "the collegiality, the chance to sit down and hash out stories, the newsroom atmosphere" (Clark 2014c). This breakdown of the newsroom culture was reinforced by Advance's emphasis on backpack journalism that encouraged journalists to be mobile and to work from the field rather than base out of the newsroom. Consequently, according to Kordalski, "all of the camaraderie and collegial 'let's work together' went out the door . . . because nobody was even in the office to have those conversations with" (Kordalski interview, March 20, 2016).

The Tension between Online and Newspaper Staffs

The strategy of moving control of the website to the media group and making it a separate company with a separate newsroom introduced both tension and competition between the two companies. According to McManamon, some *Plain Dealer* staff members expressed bitterness about the split and some have referred to the former *Plain Dealer* staff members who joined Advance Ohio as "scabs" (McManamon interview, September 29, 2015). In a *Columbia Journalism Review* article on the split into two companies, a *Plain Dealer* reporter described the relationship between the newspaper staff and the media group as "divisive" (Clark 2014c). This was echoed in interviews for this book. One reporter said the two staffs have "little or no interaction" with each other (*Plain Dealer* interview, 2015). Another reporter said, "We're not working collectively anymore because the website and the newspaper are at odds with each other"

(*Plain Dealer* interview, 2015). Another staff member described the relationship between cleveland.com and the *Plain Dealer* as "toxic" (*Plain Dealer* interview, 2016).

Adding to the tension between the two staffs was the fact that Advance did not initially invite any *Plain Dealer* photojournalists to join the Northeast Ohio Media Group. As backpack journalists, the media group's reporters were expected to attend training sessions on iPhone photography and to produce iPhone photos along with their stories. Some of the photojournalists said it made them uncomfortable when website reporters with iPhones were dispatched to the same assignments. They also felt devalued when Advance promoted the reporters' lower-quality photos and photo galleries while neglecting to promote the higher-quality work of the professionals (*Plain Dealer* interviews, 2015–2018).

Another source of tension was Advance's reorganization of the *Plain Dealer* reporting staff into teams instead of reporters working individually on specific beats (defined as regularly assigned coverage areas). In 2014 the popular court and sports beats were transferred from the newspaper staff to the website staff—and these were the beats that typically receive the most clicks online. To replace the veteran *Plain Dealer* beat reporters, Advance then hired less experienced reporters to cover them for cleveland.com. To many this was another indicator of how the *Plain Dealer* staff were being devalued by Advance, prompting one reporter to tell the *Columbia Journalism Review*: "They want us to go away. . . . If we don't have important beats, we're not going to stay" (Clark 2014a).

The tension between the newspaper and website staffs is also reinforced by the lack of public understanding of them as separate companies. An example occurred in 2014, when a video interview was conducted at the website office with three gubernatorial candidates, Governor John Kasich, Ed Fitzgerald, and Anita Rios. The interview was posted on cleveland.com shortly thereafter. However, the video, the sole event in which the three candidates expressed their positions at the same venue, remained posted to the website for only a few days. According to media critic Jim Romenesko, no one from the website would comment on the matter, including Reader Representative Diadiun. Romenesko noted that an e-mail from McManamon criticized Diadiun for refusing to comment. "That's what he's supposed to do, but since 2013 he merely has been Chris Quinn's [vice president of content for the website] apologist. He only represents NEOMG [the website], not the *Plain Dealer.* I wish I had stock in Kool-Aid" (Romenesko 2014). However, Diadiun did respond to McManamon's remarks, telling Romenesko that he had considered McManamon to be a friend and a "dedicated journalist" but that the situation had changed since the reorganization in 2013. He declined to discuss the matter further because he said he felt he was "in an untenable position and could do nothing to help the situation" (quoted in Romenesko 2014).

Design Flaws, Analytics, and Challenges

Although the Digital-First approach of giving priority to cleveland.com is central to the company's business strategy, some critics find it ironic that the Web designs for Advance newspapers are old-fashioned and somewhat dysfunctional. In an excerpt from her 2013 book on Advance, Theim quoted Joshua Benton, director of the Nieman Journalism Lab: "Their sites are among the worst in newspaper journalism. . . . They're clunky. They all look like they were built in 1998" (2013b, 144). McManamon said she finds the website's "river of news" format—which continually updates content and stacks newer content on top of older content—confusing to readers: "You have editorials flowing with news stories, feature stories with crime stories, and they're doing some of that sponsored content too, which I don't think is a very good practice . . . and stories don't stay in one place. . . . [I]t's just a jumble" (McManamon interview, February 7, 2016).

Before the Digital-First approach was instituted, McManamon said cleveland.com was considered "basically just a tool" staffed by the *Plain Dealer* that emphasized breaking news while the newspaper emphasized in-depth and investigative reporting

(McManamon interview, March 17, 2016). With Digital First, even though the newsrooms are separate, the Web staff determines the work practices and routines for both the website and the newspaper. "Now they're calling all the shots, even though we're supposed to be two different companies," she said (McManamon interview, March 17, 2016). She added that cleveland.com's control over news operations includes assigning and promoting stories that tend to get more online traffic or clicks.

This emphasis on assigning stories on the basis of online metrics or popularity has been widely criticized not only at the *Plain Dealer* but also at other metro dailies (Clark 2014b; Phillips 2014; Ryfe 2012; Lee-Wright, Phillips, and Witschge 2011). One reporter discussed an iPhone photo by an inexperienced reporter that went viral after it was published on cleveland.com. This photo, taken at an ethnic festival, included a donkey with a large penile erection. Although it garnered tens of thousands of clicks across the country, the photo's popularity had little to do with its news value (*Plain Dealer* interview, 2015). Another staff member recalled the instance in which a story on the "poop gangster," who defecated on the hoods of Cleveland police cars, went viral (*Plain Dealer* interview, 2015). Content such as this is often informally referred to as "click bait" and was encouraged by management in periodic e-mails.

Despite the fact that the newsroom had been restructured into collaborative reporting teams rather than individual reporters covering specific beats, McManamon expressed concern that the pressure to do stories that are "click bait" also promotes a sense of individual competition at the *Plain Dealer*:

> I worry that we're going to concentrate on what gets hits rather than what matters. . . . Right now they're making it very, very difficult for us because it seems like it's a competition. The media group is trying to encroach on *Plain Dealer* beats in many respects . . . and in the meantime there's all this pressure for the reporters to get clicks and page views and post galleries and all this extra work. On top of trying to be good watchdog reporters, they still

> have to figure out how to be producers. [There are] many, many challenges, but I feel our people have risen to it time and time again. (McManamon interview, September 29, 2015)

Literature on other news sites and the influence of metrics on newsroom practices echoes her concern about how this commercial imperative deters journalists from fulfilling their role to serve the public interest (Phillips 2014; Lee-Wright, Phillips, and Witschge 2011; C. Anderson 2011). C. W. Anderson is among several scholars who argue that the emphasis on metrics has resulted in less journalistic autonomy and assumes that the audience is a single aggregate rather than constituting diverse and constantly changing entities (C. Anderson 2011; Phillips 2014; Ryfe 2012; Lee-Wright, Phillips, and Witschge 2011; Witschge and Nygren 2009).

Until the elimination of the "Pub Hub" in 2019, which also meant the elimination of her job, McManamon said the most significant challenges the newspaper faced were rooted in the physical separation of the copyeditors from the writers, and the pressure to post partial stories as soon as possible, preventing reporters from having enough time to dig deeply into them. This has been especially problematic with crime stories (McManamon interview, March 17, 2016).

Because copyeditors and reporters are located in different locations,

> there's a big difference in how we do our jobs—everything is that much harder because as a copyeditor, I have to communicate to reporters either by text, or e-mail or a phone call and it makes for just a lot of extra work. I might have three or four questions when I'm working on something and I'll have to bug reporters numerous times. Whereas before I would wait till I'm done with the story, stroll over to their desk or bring them over to my desk and then improve a story that much more. It doesn't work that way now. We can't do the rewriting we might do

> before. Now we don't have the time for that. . . . And it's really something that's been bothering me, and I know it bothers the reporters who really care. (McManamon interview, March 17, 2016)

These logistical challenges were certainly compounded in 2019, when the Pub Hub staff was eliminated and copyediting and design responsibilities were outsourced to Advance's out-of-state production facility. Yet despite the challenges engendered by the newspaper's digital pivot, McManamon has continued to express pride in the work of the *Plain Dealer* reporters, their ability to cope with morale problems, and the increased workloads, as exemplified by investigative reporter Rachel Dissell.

Rachel Dissell, *Plain Dealer* Investigative Reporter

Since Dissell joined the *Plain Dealer* staff in 2002, she has been interested in stories about people and issues that are typically overlooked. Until 2014, her beat was the court system, and her articles for that beat won several investigative journalism awards. After her beat was transferred to cleveland.com, Dissell was assigned to an "enterprise team" with two other reporters, all of whom were charged with reporting on issues dealing with crime, the courts, government corruption, and social justice. The iterative reporting aspect of the Digital-First initiative has been a difficult adjustment for Dissell, who has struggled over how to "bite things out in chunks" online periodically rather than wait until she has a completed story. She said she has been experimenting with how to engage community members online without it seeming like an "artificial way of engagement" (Dissell interview).

In terms of multimedia journalism, Dissell said she was particularly pleased with her contributions to a 2015 multimedia package on a house flipping scheme for which she took some of the photos and videos as well as assuming her traditional news gathering and news writing responsibilities. However, she added that she still found it "hard to do all those multiple

Rachel Dissell, investigative reporter for the *Plain Dealer*, has less time for investigative work since the newspaper's Digital-First policy was established. (Photo by Mary Lou Nemanic, 2015.)

things at once" and said she definitely relied on the professional photojournalist with whom she was partnered for most of the visuals (Dissell interview). Despite the fact that the staff has been reduced, McManamon said the pressure to create multiple media packages became "ever more intense" in 2016 as reporters and photographers were expected to post more slideshows and photo galleries. According to Kordalski, newspaper colleagues throughout the industry agree on the difficulty in gathering facts for a story while taking photographs to depict the story visually. "It's like two different tasks at the same time. You're trying to look for two different things and it's very difficult" (Kordalski interview, March 20, 2016).

In general, Dissell said that while she occasionally produces a cell-phone video, there just is not enough time for her to post a video each day, a directive that was originally expected when the digital pivot was rolled out. Despite the challenges facing staff members to report in multiple media formats for both the website and for the newspaper, Dissell said she felt some optimism because of the "solutions journalism" approach spearheaded by their editor, George Rodrigue (Dissell interview).

George Rodrigue, *Plain Dealer* Editor

Rodrigue was hired in January 2015. His two Pulitzer Prizes for investigative journalism and his background in both newspapers and television were particularly impressive to staff members interviewed for this book. Rodrigue came to the *Plain Dealer* after serving as assistant news director at a Dallas television station. He started at the *Dallas Morning News* as a reporter in 1983, earning two Pulitzer prizes and then moving up to managing editor for a decade, during which the newsroom won a Pulitzer Prize. While he said it was a difficult decision to take on the challenges facing the *Plain Dealer,* Rodrigue took the job because he liked challenges and wanted to be in a business that cared about the community it served (Rodrigue interview).

Some staff members said they were also optimistic about Rodrigue's tenure because of his dedication to solutions journal-

George Rodrigue, who became editor of the *Plain Dealer* in 2015, instituted a solutions journalism approach to the newspaper's mission. (Photo by Mary Lou Nemanic, 2015.)

ism for the newspaper, which he described in one of his periodic columns posted on cleveland.com:

> Solutions journalism is different. Our work will be fully consistent with the core values of traditional journalism. We will remain as objective as human nature allows us to be, and use all the normal professional techniques to correct for bias. To all those traditional standards, we're adding an extra layer of focus, inquiry and effort. We're spending at least as much time seeking solutions as spotting problems. (Rodrigue 2015)

Although initially some staff members were optimistic that solutions journalism could allow the *Plain Dealer* to maintain its commitment to public service, others were less optimistic. Citing the daily posting quotas that prioritize cleveland.com over the newspaper, these staff members remained skeptical that there would be enough time or resources to devote to this time-consuming style of reportage (Plain Dealer interviews, 2015–2018). By 2019, with the elimination of the Pub Hub and with only a bare-bones staff remaining, their skepticism seems to have been affirmed, and Chittum's prediction about Advance's newspaper liquidation plan seems even more credible.

Conclusion

The *Plain Dealer* is an award-winning metro daily with a national reputation for investigative journalism that has undergone declines in circulation and in advertising like many other metro dailies struggling to survive. Yet in 2013 rather than pursuing a strategy of encouraging collaboration and integration between online and print platforms, Advance Publications abruptly established a Digital-First strategy that unleashed major changes in newsroom practices and newsroom culture. These included an emphasis on the website, a large reduction in staff, the reduction of home delivery days, and a division of its newsroom into three separate locations.

Interviews with staff members reflected the perception that Advance was more concerned about profits than its staff members as it relegated the newspaper to a secondary status, laid off so many colleagues, crammed its staff into temporary spaces, and eventually moved them to a leased space much smaller than the newsroom space for cleveland.com. A major concern was the declining journalistic standards because of the emphasis on metrics, the expectation of multimedia work, and the use of iterative writing. In addition, several staff members said they missed the newspaper's traditional collegiality as the newsroom culture dissolved under a Digital-First policy, and were anxious about the newspaper's low morale and the lack of time for the investigative work that had earned the paper its national reputation. In 2016 McManamon said, "I'm very concerned they're throwing the baby out with the bath water. The focus on in-depth stories is very uneven and there's always pressure on the staff to focus on digital when they still have a print product to produce" (McManamon interview, March 17, 2016).

In 2019, with the elimination of the Pub Hub and the reduction of the staff to just thirty, it had become apparent that her concern was well founded. As McManamon wrote in an e-mail when the company first announced it was seeking bids for an alternative to the Pub Hub, "We feel this will have a devastating impact on local journalism here, as we've seen other companies rush to this model of centralizing a very important part of what makes our paper stand out." Although Rodrigue, who took on general manager responsibilities in 2016 in addition to being editor, and was named president in 2017, had assured the public that all content decisions would remain local despite the elimination of the Pub Hub staff, the *Plain Dealer*'s newspaper guild tweeted that, on the basis of "guild conversations with Rodrigue, that does not appear to be entirely true" (Ma 2018). Heading into 2020 with a bare-bones staff, the fate of the *Plain Dealer* remained uncertain.

4

The *Buffalo News* and the *Pittsburgh Post-Gazette*

Different Strategies for Multiplatform Delivery

Unlike the *Plain Dealer*'s rapid "pivot" to Digital First, accompanied by the splits in its newsroom and its massive layoffs, two medium-sized Rust Belt metros, the *Buffalo News* and the *Pittsburgh Post-Gazette,* approached multiplatform delivery in different and less extreme ways. At the *Post-Gazette,* the transition took a decade and, according to Jon Silver, assignment editor and investigative reporter, was both "gradual and nuanced" (Silver interview, March 6, 2018). Silver noted that, by 2018, most of the staff "wholeheartedly accept[ed]" multiplatform delivery despite the initial friction between "new media adaptors" and "the dinosaurs" who were more focused on print than online journalism (Silver interviews, March 6, 2018, and August 18, 2015).

At both newspapers, staff members initially described them as multiplatform operations that featured visual journalism and that maintained a sizeable enough staff to preserve quality standards for their print editions. Over the course of this study, while this remained true for Pittsburgh, this was not the case for the *Buffalo News.* In 2017, after several years of not fully committing to online journalism, the newspaper's management accelerated its push to Digital First, emphasizing frequent postings of stories on its website and relegating print to secondary status. In 2018, a staff member noted that the "general consensus" was that the quality of the newspaper had declined as Digital First accelerated because of the continuing shrinkage of the staff through buyouts and attrition.

In contrast to Pittsburgh's consistent transition to multiplatform delivery, at the *Buffalo News* several staff members described the transition as extremely difficult, slow, and sporadic. Although for many years the *News* had a website, most of that time it was considered supplementary to print; consequently, until recent years its digital delivery was less developed than many metros across the country (*Buffalo News* interviews, 2015–2018). However, in 2017, the *Buffalo News* shifted to a Digital-First approach that required the staff to post all content online first while frequently updating these stories and giving priority to online work over that of the newspaper (Connolly interview, August 2, 2017). This reorientation was so digitally centric that stories were sometimes withheld from print for two to three days (Connolly interview, August 2, 2017). This Digital-First shift was instituted at a time when the staff had been reduced to fewer than one hundred through buyouts and attrition. By 2018 the newsroom size had dropped to fewer than fifty, less than one-quarter of its size of more than two hundred in the early 2000s (Fink 2018).

Notwithstanding their differences, these two metro dailies still have many traits in common. Both the *Buffalo News* and the *Pittsburgh Post-Gazette* earned national reputations for excellent journalism, as evidenced by the Pulitzer Prizes they have been awarded, along with other national and regional awards. Both have invested in and continue to support in-depth and investigative work, which is particularly impressive because so many metro dailies have eliminated long-term stories in favor of briefs and breaking news posts (Starkman 2014; Phillips 2014). In addition, both newspapers are genuinely committed to visual journalism across platforms. Both the *Buffalo News* and the *Pittsburgh Post-Gazette* are also known for their strong connections to the communities they serve and their commitments to public service. In both cases staff members spoke highly of their supervising editors because of management's continued support for quality reporting standards and emphasis on visual journalism and because of their willingness to experiment as they transitioned into multiplatform delivery.

The *Buffalo News* and Berkshire Hathaway

The *Buffalo News* is the primary newspaper for the Buffalo-Niagara region of 1.3 million and has been recognized with major journalism awards, including four Pulitzer Prizes. Founded by Edward H. Butler, it was first published in 1880 as a Sunday-only newspaper, but over time the *Buffalo Evening News* became one of a few daily newspapers serving western New York. Its primary competition was a morning newspaper, the *Buffalo Courier Express.* In 1977 the *Buffalo Evening News* was purchased by Warren Buffett's Berkshire Hathaway Company. When the *Courier Express* closed in 1982, the newspaper's name was shortened to the *Buffalo News,* and it began publishing both morning and afternoon editions. In 2006 it became a morning-only newspaper.

Berkshire Hathaway is run by its CEO, billionaire investor Warren Buffett, who purchased the *Buffalo News* in 1977 for $32.5 million. By the early 2000s the newspaper had made more than $750 million in pre-tax revenue. Rather than focusing on short-term profits as corporate owners so often do, Buffett has typically taken the long-term view on his investments to ensure a quality product, and in the case of the daily news operations at the *Buffalo News,* has taken a hands-off management approach (Miles 2002).

In his biography of Buffett, Robert Miles describes Buffett's long-term perspective on profitability as a "buy and hold investment" strategy that includes allowing managers to set policies and run the day-to-day operations of the newspaper (2002, 140). Miles also details Buffett's concern for quality, as reflected in his management style. "We really do not think as much about the short term. . . . We do not focus on quarterly results. . . . What we're focused on in the long term is building the value of

According to Brian Connolly, vice president of innovation and business development for the *Buffalo News*, key reader engagement strategies include emphasizing both watchdog journalism and visual journalism. (Photo by Mary Lou Nemanic, 2015.)

our businesses. And that can only be measured by net income" (Miles 2002, 147).

Notably under Buffett's leadership the *Buffalo News* has not had the periodic layoffs or reductions in resources that many metro dailies have suffered. However, newsroom numbers have been reduced through buyouts and attrition. According to Buffalo Newspaper Guild member Mark Sommer, "It's helped that we haven't had layoffs, had our benefits slashed or seen the other kinds of cuts so many papers have had" (Sommer 2016). Guild president Sandy Tan echoed this: "We're lucky to work for Berkshire Hathaway. It could be lot worse. . . . If you look at the *Buffalo News* and compare it to other news organizations, the *Buffalo News* is much more stable and more fortunate than other newspapers. We're not owned by a company that lays off people and cuts resources" (Tan interview).

According to Vice President for Innovation and Business Development Brian Connolly, a major reason the *News* is "unique" is its "local control over the paper. We're not a part of a chain, we have a fantastic owner, and as long as we're keeping the business a viable business, we get to call the shots" (Connolly interview, August 2, 2017).

Even with continual declines in advertising revenue, the *Buffalo News* was still profitable through most of 2017. The *News* has been in a more stable position than many other metro dailies because it is one of the "higher penetration newspapers in the country," with an older, very loyal readership base, according to Connolly (Connolly interview, December 15, 2015).

> Although the industry continues to be challenged, we continue to do better than most of our peers by the metrics of staying profitable and being able to maintain a robust news operation. Obviously, we have the benefit of great ownership that does not put on us the pressure that all of the chains have. (Connolly interview, August 2, 2017)

Connolly also added that the paper has the "benefit of great readership and we continue to deliver them a great product" (Connolly interview, August 2, 2017). Cathaleen Curtiss, director of photography, echoed Connolly's assessment of the readers of the *Buffalo News.* "Buffalo is a newspaper town," and reading the newspaper is part of many residents' daily routines, she said (Curtiss interview).

However, according to media analyst Rem Rieder, as the annual declines in advertising and circulation have continued to eat away at the newspaper industry's profit margins, Warren Buffett has begun to sound "decidedly less bullish" about the future of print, raising concerns that the newspaper might be sold (Rieder 2016b). Nonetheless, Buffett admits he still loves newspapers, telling Rieder, "We would never sell a newspaper. . . . I want to be the last guy standing."

Strengths of the *Buffalo News*

Besides "fantastic ownership," Connolly also attributed the newspaper's continuing success to "great writing" and its emphasis on visual journalism (Connolly interview, August 2, 2017). Despite the additional responsibilities of its website, the newspaper has continued to maintain its reputation for investigative and in-depth journalism even though this is a long-term investment that many metro dailies have abandoned as their staffs have been reduced and their multiplatform duties have expanded.

"Right now, we have a lot of what we call watchdog journalism. We have reporters who are bird-dogging the criminal justice system and in the realm of politics and campaign finance and those sorts of things. . . . We definitely have a commitment to that regardless of how those stories do" in terms of their popularity (Connolly interview, August 2, 2017). Connolly's comment reflects Buffalo's emphasis on public service over metrics, a balancing act that many metros are struggling with as their emphasis on getting hits increasingly preoccupies the industry (Starkman 2014; C. Anderson 2011; Witschge and Nygren 2009).

Typical of staff comments on the strengths of the *Buffalo News* were those of digital news editor Sara Meehan, who highlighted the newspaper's "really strong reporters, who are extremely good at breaking news and at long-form. . . . [W]e have good writers who can make you think" (Meehan interview). One of those writers, Tim O'Shei, had freelanced as feature writer for the newspaper and was eventually hired full time in 2014 to work on long-term feature projects. O'Shei said he considers himself extremely fortunate to be able to devote long periods of time on his stories (O'Shei interview). Unlike other metros that have typically cut back on long-term original reporting projects, the *Buffalo News* gives him ample time for in-depth work. Working on his own story ideas as well as assigned stories, O'Shei said he is encouraged "to have the time to do a great job . . . and to make a big impact" (O'Shei interview).

Having adjusted to multiplatform delivery, *Buffalo News* business reporter and columnist Samantha Christmann regularly uses social media to promote her stories and columns. (Photo by Mary Lou Nemanic, 2015.)

Samantha Christmann's situation is more typical than O'Shei's. Christmann is a business reporter and columnist who joined the newspaper in 2008. That year she launched her column, the Discount Diva, to help consumers save money during the recession. Occasionally Christmann gets the opportunity to do long-term projects, but most of her daily work involves writing several online posts as she works on more detailed print stories (Christmann interviews, December 15, 2015; May 17, 2016; and February 25, 2018). Christmann said she has adapted to writing iteratively—or writing in chunks that are updated and uploaded frequently—and she often uses social media to promote her stories. While Christmann said she has enjoyed writing for the website, she is concerned at times that a story on the opening of a new Sonic restaurant may get many more hits than a serious business story on which she has worked for six months (Christmann interview, May 17, 2016). Although she can see the pitfalls of analytics, Christmann wrote in an e-mail that she has also gained an appreciation for them:

> There were stories I used to pitch to my editor that never got any traction. They would get dismissed or just completely misunderstood. I have more freedom to try different things now, and I get to try more of those ideas. All those years my story ideas got rejected, I assumed I just had bad instincts. But now, with analytics, I have something that shows there are a lot of people out there who want to read those stories I've always wanted to write. I can show my editor that I know what I'm doing. When I pitch a story, I have something to back it up. I can show that a topic I'm interested in interests other people, too. That it's worth writing about. A lot of those stories are the most read story of the day, the week, or the month. And other stories that an editor might have insisted on in the past, something I dreaded writing, might get fewer than five hundred views. Stories that would've been dismissed before now make the front page. I'm regularly writing more of what I want and less of what I don't. I have more confidence in myself as a writer. . . . I think maybe I was parroting a lot of people's fears about analytics before. I do think it's important not to let them steer the ship, but I have found tremendous value in Parse.ly and Metrics for News.

Also very active online, especially on social media, is Digital Content Coordinator Ben Tsujimoto. Tsujimoto assigns stories and edits content for buffalo.com. He said he considers driving traffic to the newspaper's website as one of his major responsibilities, especially through social media. He regularly utilizes a program called Echo Box that automates the distribution of social media content by sending out Tweets and Facebook posts at optimal times to reach the largest audiences (Tsujimoto interview, March 5, 2018).

Visual Journalism Emphasis

Another key strategy for sustaining the success of the *Buffalo News* emphasized by Vice President Brian Connolly is visual journalism. In a decade when entire photo staffs are being cut in favor of reporters with iPhones, the *Buffalo News* has maintained a photo staff of seven, and in 2016 even added to its staff by hiring a director of photography, Cathaleen Curtiss. Curtiss said she believes maintaining a substantial photo staff is a critical element for newspapers if they want to be successful across platforms. She also emphasized experimenting with new initiatives such as A Photo a Day, an online feature that posts engaging no-news photos by *Buffalo News* photographers as a challenge to readers "to look at things differently, to remind us all to slow down and enjoy our surroundings" (Curtiss interview; *Buffalo News,* 2018). In addition, although the newspaper has found that its photos and photo galleries are very popular with its readers, Curtiss said that after experimenting with video and finding it to be unpopular, the paper has moved away from video production with plans to revisit video in the future (Curtiss interview).

Curtiss said she appreciates the support for visual journalism from editor and vice president Mike Connelly and from Vice President Brian Connolly when so many metros have drastically reduced their photo staffs (Curtiss interview). Brian Connolly noted that the newspaper has demonstrated its commitment to photojournalism by protecting the size of the photojournalism staff, investing "in the best equipment possible," and hiring Curtiss for the new position of director of photography (Connolly interview, August 2, 2017).

In addition to creating a position for Curtiss, Connolly said the newspaper's purchase of a drone for aerial photography, along with investing in insurance and training for Curtiss and another photojournalist to use it, also highlights the newspaper's commitment to visual journalism. He added that the drone has enabled the paper to publish "spectacular photography, and it's not just 'look at this new trick we have up our sleeves' but is really useful journalistically to illustrate stories" (Connolly interview,

In 2017 *Buffalo News* chief photographer Derek Gee used a drone to capture this panoramic photograph of the Buffalo skyline covered in blue light in honor of a slain police officer. (Photo by Derek Gee. With permission of *The Buffalo News*.)

August 2, 2017). This was evident in November 2017, when the staff produced a special eight-page edition on the funeral of a slain police officer. A drone was used for the lead photograph, a panorama of the Buffalo skyline covered in blue light in tribute to the officer. This edition was produced as a "live print package," which was distributed to those who attended the funeral *as they left* the service (Burton 2017).

Management's support for experimentation in storytelling methods and platforms was another key element identified by the staff as integral to the newspaper's continuing success. Particularly innovative is the work of data-driven enterprise editor/reporter Patrick Lakamp, who heads up a team of six reporters engaged in a relatively new area of visual journalism known as data visualization. This involves quantitative reporting techniques utilizing statistical and information graphics to present data.

Challenges Facing the *Buffalo News*

Despite all its strengths and its innovative ethos, the *Buffalo News* still struggles with many of the same challenges facing the newspaper industry in general. Its newsroom, like so many other metro newsrooms, has shrunk considerably as the industry has become less profitable while transitioning to multiplatform delivery. In 2015, when this study of the *Buffalo News* began, there were approximately 135 staff members in the newsroom (Connolly interview, December 15, 2015; *Buffalo News* interviews, 2018). In 2017 Connolly had estimated the newsroom to be at 119 or 120, including part-time staff members. And although he characterized the newsroom as a "robust operation," its size was down from a peak of more than 200 in the early 2000s (Connolly interview, August 2, 2017; Sullivan interview). By June 2018 that number had dropped to approximately 84 after another round of both voluntary and forced or "targeted" buyouts (Tan interview). Targeted buyouts involve positions that were eliminated, such as those on the copy desk, which the *Buffalo News* abolished entirely. Staff members who took targeted buyouts avoided being reassigned "into unknown or dramatically different job duties" (Buffalo Newspaper Guild 2018). By late July 2018, additional buyouts reduced the staff to 44 (Fink 2018).

The concern for newsroom shrinkage was a major challenge emphasized by several veteran and former staff members because responsibilities for online work were added to their print responsibilities at a time when downsized staff had not received raises in seven years. In 2017 the Buffalo Newspaper Guild reported that the staff finally received a raise of just under 3 percent in exchange for contributing more for their health care premiums (Tan interview). As the staff diminished and more responsibilities were added to accommodate the 24/7 demands of the Web, several staff members described the increasing difficulty in keeping pace with breaking news and the demands of the print edition. Connolly also emphasized the difficulty of multiplatform work as a "balancing act" between print and online (Connolly interview, December 15, 2015). One staff member's comment summed up the sense of frustration and the newsroom's declining morale: "People are just cranking out the work. . . . [H]ow much more can we be expected to do?" (*Buffalo News* interview, 2015).

While acknowledging the pressure that having both online and print responsibilities puts on the newspaper staff, Connolly explained in 2017 that the newsroom numbers did not tell the whole story, since there have been some hires in strategic areas. "Through attrition we've lost people, but we've also hired. I'm sure we're down, I'd guess somewhere between five and ten positions since you [referring to me] visited in the newsroom in 2015." He added: "We are still hiring but it's no longer [that] somebody leaves and you automatically replace that position. . . . We've been more strategic about the hires. . . . [A]s somebody leaves, we reevaluate whether that position needs to be filled or there's a new need on the staff" (Connolly interview, August 2, 2017).

Digital-First Issues

In 2018, some staff members expressed frustration that the accelerated push to Digital-First was coming at a time when staff numbers were at a new low after so many years of hesitating to embrace digital delivery, and that it was coming at the expense of the print product, which had declined in quality as well as in size. One staff member described how the new strategy had contributed to the decline: "It's definitely Digital First for everything. In fact, what they kind of say is 'Everything is the Web, and the paper will fill itself. We'll take the best of the Web and put it in the paper.' But it's almost like the paper is sort of an afterthought" (*Buffalo News* interview, 2018).

In assessing the paper's transition to multiplatform delivery, Lakamp characterized it as slow and difficult, with resistance from long-time staff members who were influenced by habits from the print-only newsroom culture and who either were not able to embrace multiplatform practices that readily, or found them too difficult to master (Lakamp interview). David Ryfe's book *Can Journalism Survive?* (2012) identified this problem in his research accounts of metros back in 2004 and 2005. Ryfe found that a number of veteran staff members were not only slow to adapt to the Web but also resistant to it. This was because of ingrained printcentric habits and because of a common bias against the Web as a place where many felt the accuracy and balance of quality journalism were overshadowed by the race to be the first to post content online (Ryfe 2012).

Tsujimoto was even more emphatic about the continuing difficulty of the transition because of what he described as the

> strong reluctance of a lot of people who are creating the content to actually embrace the digital approach. And I don't think that can be overstated. That's definitely an issue in the newsroom now. . . . [T]he 800-pound gorilla [in the room] is that you have to change the way you work and change what you cover and be willing to try a whole lot of different things, but there's a mentality that the things that you are doing with the news [are] making money . . . and the print product is still what you're going to do even though there's this increasing demand on the outside to actually change. So, it's fighting the habit[s] [and] instincts from before. (Tsujimoto interview, June 9, 2016)

In 2016 another staff member also characterized the ongoing transition to digital delivery as both challenging and slow but did not feel the staff who were not digitally oriented were intentionally reluctant. "I think we started doing it much later than a lot of other publications. There was resistance, not outright resistance, but people just not getting it, not understanding it. We still have quite a few people who just don't get the idea, and who, despite their efforts, just don't know how to think that way" (*Buffalo News* interview, 2016).

Other staff members echoed this frustration that the push to multiplatform delivery was delayed until about 2017, and that the Digital-First policy was initiated too rapidly. One staff member explained that prior to 2017 they were required "to think digital first" yet were still expected "to focus on print" (*Buffalo News* interview, 2016). This neglect of a well-developed multiplatform policy is a common problem in the transitions detailed in ethnographic and case studies in scholarly and professional literature on newspapers, particularly the work of Scott Reinardy (2016) and Michael Shapiro, Anna Hiatt, and Mike Hoyt (2015). In addition, as emphasized in this literature, the lack of clear-cut multiplatform policies, along with the lack of training in multiplatform delivery, has taken its toll on newsroom morale across the industry as staff members try to "do more with less."

Although he acknowledged that the transition to multiplatform delivery has been "slow," Connolly maintained that this "kept us from hurting ourselves in ways that are difficult to recover from" (Connolly interview, August 2, 2017). This reticence to fully transition to multiplatform delivery is reflected in the philosophy of the newspaper's long-time publisher, Stan Lipsey, who was quoted in a biography on Warren Buffett:

> I always like to see the other guy break paths . . . and if I can come in late, I will. I tell my people that sometimes the smartest decision you can make is to do nothing. I don't like being a pioneer, and I won't be one unless I see an opportunity where the first guy is going to benefit, and I watch that very closely. (Miles 2002, 248)

Until his retirement in 2012, Lipsey's influence meant digital delivery would be not be a priority, although some staff members identified former editor and vice president Margaret Sullivan as a counterforce to this disinclination. Christmann said that before Sullivan left that same year, Sullivan had made substantial efforts to settle labor issues impeding advances in the newspaper's online delivery (Christmann interview, December 15, 2015; Sullivan interview). Christmann, who was mentored by Sullivan, said that despite the very limited time available for training, she was impressed that Sullivan had also brought video professionals into the newsroom to train the staff (Christmann interview, December 15, 2015).

Despite Sullivan's efforts, the momentum for multiplatform delivery did not intensify until the push for Digital First, which relegated print to a secondary position. Christmann described the Digital-First policy as requiring that all stories be posted online first, whether or not they were breaking news stories. In addition, she recalled the staff was told:

> We are no longer a newspaper of record. There are going to be a lot of little stories we would have reported in the past that we are just going to let go now. Now we're going to be focusing on enterprise stories where we're the only people that have them. So, we want to use our time wisely to do the enterprise reporting rather than trying to get every single thing that happens on the record of the paper. (Christmann interview, May 17, 2016)

Consequently, with Digital First, Christmann was required to post five to six brief stories per day instead of writing two to four stories per day. Although the shorter pieces did not take as much time to write, she explained that producing the stories was more time intensive because she had to gather the information for one to four additional stories each day (Christmann interview, May 17, 2016).

Through most of 2017 staff members often expressed pride in the quality of the print product, with some describing the *Buffalo News* as the best metro of its size in the country. However, in late 2017 some staff members began expressing concerns that print quality was declining because Digital-First's implementation involved reducing the number of print pages and using template-based layouts in which brief stories harvested from the website were automatically inserted into print page layouts (*Buffalo News* interviews, 2017–2018). One staff member called the content of these web-harvested briefs for print "garbage." Some staff members were also disappointed that content posted online was sometimes withheld from print for two to three days. These staff members generally expressed frustration and disappointment that the newsroom had been downsized so much that the newspaper had to focus on digital at the expense of print rather than take a multiplatform approach. Some staff members also expressed concern about the elimination of the copy desk in favor of departmental editors and reporters doing the copyediting. This has resulted in more errors and typos appearing in print and online (*Buffalo News* interviews, 2017 and 2018).

In general, it should be noted that, despite a lack of an integrated approach to multiplatform delivery, staff members stated that digital delivery was improving since the website was redesigned and that the newspaper was having success with a new paywall-protected website with exclusive content related to the Buffalo Bills of the National Football League. In addition, staff members continued to express pride in their investigative reporting and visual journalism as distinctive in the industry and as key elements for their newspaper's future viability. Nonetheless, they continued to express concern about not only their shrinking newsroom but also the Trump administration's tariffs on imports of Canadian paper, which raised costs by one-third and led to a shortage of newsprint in 2017 (Connelly 2018).

The *Pittsburgh Post-Gazette* and Block Communications

In 1786 a four-page weekly, the *Pittsburgh Gazette,* became the first newspaper published west of the Alleghenies. It covered the inception of the United States, even publishing the entire U.S. Constitution shortly after its adoption. In 1833 the *Gazette* became a daily paper and over the years competed with and merged with other metro papers in Pittsburgh. During the 1920s publisher Paul Block gained control of four of Pittsburgh's five papers and in 1927 began publishing the *Pittsburgh Post-Gazette.* In 1989, Block's grandsons, Allan and John Robinson Block, became co-publishers, and John assumed the duties of editor in chief. Over time the *Pittsburgh Post-Gazette* has attained national prominence with awards for its journalism and photojournalism, including five Pulitzer Prizes. Serving a metro area of about 2.3 million people, until 2016 it was one of the few metro dailies with a metro-area rival. Starting in the early 1990s its chief competitor was a conservative paper, the *Pittsburgh Tribune-Review,* but in 2016, after laying off more than 150 employees, the *Tribune-Review* ceased print publication and became a digital-only news provider. In 2018, to cut back on its losses and focus more on its digital platforms, the *Pittsburgh Post-Gazette* reduced its publication days from seven to five, becoming the largest U.S. city without a daily newspaper, according to media analyst Ken Doctor (quoted in Deppen 2018b). In 2019 publication days were reduced to three days a week.

Challenges Facing the *Pittsburgh Post-Gazette*

In 2015, to address financial problems from advertising losses and an outdated and underutilized newsroom because its staff had been reduced through attrition and buyouts, the newspaper sold its building in a prime section of the downtown area and relocated just north of downtown. As detailed in Chapter 1, the *Post-Gazette*'s commitment to multiplatform news is evident

The *Pittsburgh Post-Gazette*'s newsroom was custom designed to foster collaboration and promote multiplatform delivery. (Photo by Mary Lou Nemanic, 2015.)

in its distinctive new newsroom design created by the architect for the *Toronto Globe and Mail* (Shribman interview, August 8, 2015). The open-plan configuration, with an editing hub at its center, was designed to facilitate collaboration and to emphasize multiplatform content delivery, according to executive editor David Shribman. Shribman also pointed out that the new newsroom design expresses a sense of optimism and an emphasis on looking toward the future (Coester 2017).

Overall, staff members, editors, and former staff members interviewed typically expressed positive assessments of the newspaper's transition from print-only to multiplatform delivery. In addition, former deputy managing editor Mila Sanina credited Shribman's leadership as crucial to the newspaper's viability, describing him as "protecting the newsroom" and being "very good at managing the politics of it while walling the newsroom out" (Sanina interview, March 5, 2018). Assignment editor Jon Silver reinforced this assessment, crediting Shribman with figuring out "how to live within the budget and live well" (Silver interview, March 6, 2018). Shribman asserted that the *Post-Gazette*'s staff has transitioned fully into multimedia journalism, noting in 2016 that he could identify only a few print-only individuals who remained on staff (Shribman interview, October 21, 2016).

Despite many years of declines in annual profits, Shribman said the newspaper has survived because it offers quality journalism and because of the "forbearance" of the Block family, which owns it (Shribman interview, August 8, 2015). Media analysts attribute the *Post-Gazette*'s success to not only support from its ownership but also a loyal core of readers who still make the newspaper profitable, though by only a small margin compared to its peak years (Doctor 2015a; Silver interview, March 6, 2018).

Despite Shribman's positive assessment of the Block family's support of the newspaper, a schism between the staff and Block had been growing over several years as Block increasingly interjected his political and racial views into *Post-Gazette* editorials. In January 2018 this situation erupted into a public controversy when Block insisted the *Post-Gazette* publish an editorial defending President Donald Trump's racist comments on immigration (Fuoco 2018a; Calderone 2018; Deitch 2018; Cillizza 2018). The editorial, entitled "Reason as Racism," which originally ran in the *Toledo Blade*, was published in Pittsburgh on the Martin Luther King Jr. holiday. It asserted that calling people racist is "the new McCarthyism," and it defended President Donald Trump's reported comments that the United States should accept immigrants from white countries such as Norway instead of "shithole countries" like Haiti or "Africa." In a *Politico* article, Michael Calderone included excerpts from the editorial: "'It is not racist to say that this country cannot take only the worst people from the worst places and that we want some of the best people from the best places, many of which are inhabited by people of color,' the editorial read. 'That's not racism, it is reason'" (Calderone 2018).

The Newspaper Guild of Pittsburgh, representing 150 employees, vehemently disagreed. In a letter to the editor, the guild wrote that its members were "collectively appalled and crestfallen by the repugnant editorial. . . . As a matter of course, the Guild does not weigh in on editorial positions, but this piece is so extraordinary in its mindless, sycophantic embrace of racist values and outright bigotry espoused by this country's president that we would be morally, journalistically, and humanly remiss not to speak out against it" (Fuoco 2018a).

Although the *Post-Gazette* did not run the letter to the editor, it was circulated online and received attention in the national press (Fuoco 2018a; Calderone 2018). Adding to the guild's denunciations came condemnations from two of Pittsburgh's leading foundations, the Heinz Endowments and the Pittsburgh Foundation. In an online statement, they called the editorial "an embarrassment to Pittsburgh" and a "cover for racist rhetoric." The statement was displayed beneath an illustration of large black letters against a white wall spelling the word "SHAME" (Oliphant and King 2018). A press release from the Pittsburgh Black Media Federation also condemned the editorial, as did a letter from more than two dozen former *Post-Gazette* staff members (Fuoco 2018a; Calderone 2018).

While the *Post-Gazette* did not publish the guild's letter, it did publish a letter from sixteen Block family members and BCI shareholders who called the editorial an attempt "to justify blatant racism" and a perspective that was not representative of the progressive values of the late, revered *Post-Gazette* publisher William Block Sr., John Robinson Block's uncle (Fuoco 2018a; Calderone 2018).

Ongoing labor issues have made this controversy even more disconcerting and added to the deflation of newsroom morale. According to an article in the *Columbia Journalism Review* by Michael Fuoco, reporter and president of the Newspaper Guild of Pittsburgh:

> We already were embroiled on several fronts with Block and the family-owned Block Communications, Inc. . . . Because of that, we were acutely aware of where John Robinson Block and his twin brother, Allan Block, BCI's chairman and editorial supporter, stood on social and economic justice issues. Our contract expired March 31; for the past 12 years, we've had a pay cut of at least 10 percent, and negotiations with BCI's union-busting law firm, King and Ballow of Nashville, have become increasingly contentious. We recently filed an Unfair Labor Practice charge against the company for violating federal law by unilaterally changing our health-care benefits in the midst of ongoing, albeit glacial, bargaining. Media stories about the charge appeared the same day as the editorial. (Fuoco 2018a)

In addition, Fuoco wrote that, during the same time period, the guild was defending a member who had warned the public through the *Post-Gazette*'s Twitter account, "Our publisher is requesting us to remove @realDonaldTrump's 'vulgar language' from the lede in our @AP story about his vulgar language" (Fuoco 2018a). Nevertheless, the story remained on the website with no change; the next day, however, the vulgar expression had been censored out of the newspaper's AP lead, appearing only in the jump (Fuoco 2018a). Although this could be written off as a minor incident, it raised big concerns among the staff about journalistic autonomy at the *Post-Gazette*, concerns echoed in the literature on the status of journalism worldwide (*Pittsburgh Post-Gazette* interviews, 2018; Phillips 2014; Lee-Wright, Phillips, and Witschge 2011).

Exacerbating the tension between the staff and the publisher were two changes Block made to the *Post-Gazette*'s editorial board. In March 2018 he announced he was merging the editorial boards of the *Pittsburgh Post-Gazette* and the *Toledo Blade* and that Block had appointed Keith Burris, who had written the "Reason as Racism" editorial, as editor, vice president, and editorial director for Block newspapers (*Pittsburgh Post-Gazette* 2018). In an article on the *Post-Gazette*'s website, Burris (2018) wrote: "For all of us, this is going to be fun. The trick will be to make our pages fun for our readers, with meaningful and compelling commentary on local, state, national, international and cultural topics."

In response, *Pittsburgh City Paper*'s Charlie Deitch (2018) wrote:

> The recent editorial stance of the *Post-Gazette* has turned off many of its loyal readers. The paper's news-gathering organization is as good as it ever was. The problem is, people are getting turned off, and not just by the paper's opinions, but also by the smug, tone-deaf way it's being shoved in their faces. Putting Keith Burris in charge is only adding fuel to the fire.

According to Silver, in 2018 the editorials published in the *Pittsburgh Post-Gazette* were "the product of a single individual, the publisher," adding that the newspaper's editorial board lacked the diversity of past years in terms of the inclusion of women or people of color (Silver interview, March 6, 2018). Originally the *Post-Gazette*'s editorial board determined the editorial positions of the newspaper in conjunction with its mission, published online in 2008:

> The Post-Gazette Editorial Board determines the viewpoint of the newspaper as an institution and as a long-standing community leader in Western Pennsylvania. Its opinions are expressed in editorials, the unsigned commentaries that appear on the website and down the left side of the printed editorial page. Although written by individuals, *the editorials carry no bylines because they represent the consensus of the group on key public policy issues, candidates seeking election and major events of the day.* The board meets daily to choose the subjects for comment and to discuss the positions the Post-Gazette should take. Members of the editorial board include John Robinson Block, publisher and editor-in-chief; John Allison, editorial page editor; associate editor Dan Simpson; and associate editor Joe Smydo. [The statement was signed by John Robinson Block, publisher and editor-in-chief, and dated June 19, 2008.] (Block 2008, emphasis added)

In contrast to the new direction of the *Post-Gazette*'s editorial board, typically metro daily editorial boards comprise several editors who publish editorials based on a consensus on issues relating to the context of the metro areas they cover (Lyons 2018b). At the *Post-Gazette,* the change in editorial policy has been a source of frustration and consternation for the staff because of the public perception that editorials are written by the reporting staff. Consequently, as photojournalist Stephanie Strasburg noted:

> I think one of the biggest challenges for the *Post-Gazette* is the morale because of what's happening with our editorial department and what's happening with the union negotiations that seem like never ending. . . . What's happening with the editorial department is really hard for somebody who takes great pride in being a community journalist . . . and I feel like people want to bring

> up those editorials at almost every assignment I go to. It's really heartbreaking because we as storytellers have really placed value and have placed time in going out and building relationships with the community and making sure we're telling the stories about the parts of the community that otherwise don't get covered . . . and all of that can be taken away just like that. . . . It's shortsighted for our editorial department to not realize how this affects their colleagues and employees in the field and how it doesn't represent the majority of what the city that they cover thinks. (Strasburg interview)

Adding even more fuel to the fire was the editorial board's 2018 endorsement of Rick Saccone, a conservative Republican candidate for the Eighteenth Congressional District and a strong Trump supporter. The endorsement was based on the rationale that Saccone had greater legislative experience than his opponent, Conor Lamb, and also because of fears that a Democratic victory would lead to President Trump's impeachment (Smith 2018). Backlash to the endorsement emerged quickly, and concern for the editorial board's conservative-leaning orientation continued to garner national coverage and the cancellation of hundreds of subscriptions (Lyons 2018b; Sheehan 2018).

Several staff members interviewed for this book and quoted in news articles were baffled about why Block, who had been known as an advocate of the *Post-Gazette* despite its diminishing profits and "who rarely weighs in on the content of news pages," had increasingly dominated the newspaper's editorial board with positions that ran counter to the progressive ethos of the city and the newspaper's staff (Lakshmanan 2018). Interestingly, Block was once described in the *American Journalism Review* as someone who had worked as a journalist and was committed to the public service role of the *Post-Gazette,* arguing "passionately for putting journalistic merit over the bottom line" (Enda 2006).

Additional concerns about the *Post-Gazette*'s editorial page emerged in June 2018 when the editorial cartoonist, Rob Rogers, was fired after twenty-five years at the newspaper. This occurred after Burris rejected nineteen ideas or drafts of cartoons and Rogers posted some of them on his Facebook page, gaining national attention (Rogers 2018; Lyons 2018a; Devega 2018). His termination triggered condemnations of the paper by Pittsburgh's mayor and the Newspaper Guild of Pittsburgh. In addition, the newspaper staff and eighteen managers, including Shribman, purchased advertising space in the *Post-Gazette* to alert the public to the fact that the newsroom is a separate operation from the editorial pages and to discourage readers from canceling their subscriptions (Gannon 2018). Rogers's firing also led to the offer of an exhibition of Rogers's censored cartoons in Washington, DC (Cavna 2018).

Protracted Negotiations and Charges of Union Busting

Adding to the decline in morale at the *Pittsburgh Post-Gazette* were the ongoing and contentious labor negotiations between the newspaper guild and the law firm of King and Ballow representing BCI. This firm was known for its union-busting tactics that involved deliberately prolonging negotiations to discredit the union (Fuoco 2018b). In January 2018, because their contract had expired on March 31, 2017, and negotiations were stalled, the newspaper guild established a mobilization effort in the form of a byline strike. In an article on the Newspaper Guild of Pittsburgh's website, Fuoco described this as a campaign to withhold the bylines of writers, reporters, and photographers from the print and online versions of the newspaper to alert "the public of contentious contract talks that threaten the operation of the 231-year-old Pittsburgh institution" (Fuoco 2018b). Fuoco framed the negotiations around the issue of economic justice, writing in March 2018 that over the previous twelve years

> guild members have earned 10 percent less than in 2006, pensions have been frozen, benefits have been cut[,] health-care coverage has decreased. Yet the cost of

> everything—including the Pittsburgh Post-Gazette—has increased dramatically. Still, over the last 10 months, in some of the most contentious contract talks at the paper in history, the company is demanding even more give-backs. It is true that the *Post-Gazette*, like most newspapers in the country, loses money. But its highly profitable parent company BCI is able to write off those losses and regularly earns more than $100 million in profits annually. While the Guild typically keeps negotiations confidential, BCI's refusal to move off its draconian proposal has forced us to go public. (Fuoco 2018b)

Despite morale problems related to ongoing contract negotiations and concerns about journalistic autonomy and Block's domination of the editorial board, Silver nonetheless remained passionate about his work, emphasizing that the staff was still focused on quality journalism, and noting, "We put out a kick-ass paper every day!" (Silver interview, March 6, 2018). Significantly, although Silver was concerned about newsroom shrinkage, his major concerns in 2018 related to labor negotiations and issues with the editorial board. Although the staff of approximately 150 is about half what the newsroom size was during its peak years, its shrinkage has been relatively gradual, implemented mostly through buyouts and even punctuated by occasional hires for digital positions (Silver interview, March 6, 2018). In addition, Silver estimated that there were approximately 20–24 managers outside of the guild membership, bringing the newsroom numbers to approximately 170–175.

> I think we have net-grown in the last couple years. . . . [W]e've had a fair amount of turnovers and a fair amount of hiring over the last few years, which sounds like it doesn't make any sense. . . . We exist in an unusual bubble honestly. There are very quirky dynamics at work in the family ownership structure and things that just do not make sense economically, fiscally. . . . [I]t's like we're in a parallel universe. (Silver interview, March 6, 2018)

Jon Silver, assignment editor, investigative reporter, and unit chairman of the newspaper guild—though concerned about newsroom morale in light of racist editorials and protracted labor negotiations—remains passionate about the *Post-Gazette*. (Photo by Mary Lou Nemanic, 2015.)

Citing the purchase of a new printing press a few years prior and the continual authorization of new hires, Silver noted that the newspaper was very fortunate that it did not suffer the kind of shrinkage typical of metros throughout the industry, much of which he credited to Shribman's budgetary savvy (Silver interview, March 6, 2018).

Silver joined the *Pittsburgh Post-Gazette* staff in 1996 first as a reporter and since 2016 as an assignment editor who oversees a team of reporters covering public safety, the courts, the police, and enterprise reporting (Silver interview, March 6, 2018). Enterprise reporting involves stories generated by the reporters themselves rather than by press releases or current news topics. Although Silver said he has "mixed feelings" about moving away from writing on a daily basis and from "face time with interesting people and events," he said he enjoys working with reporters and helping them develop their story ideas (Silver interview, March 6, 2018). For the past ten years, Silver has also been heavily involved in union activities as the newspaper guild's unit chairman. In 2018 he said he was particularly concerned about the staff's low morale because of protracted contract negotiations and because of the domination of the editorial board by Block, whose ultraconservative values neither reflected those of the staff nor the progressive ethos of the City of Pittsburgh.

Former deputy managing editor Mila Sanina agreed with this view, noting that the editorial board had lost sight of its mission to serve its readers. She added that the editorial page had become a "racist, bigoted platform" for Block's personal opinions (Sanina interview, March 5, 2018). Sanina left the *Post-Gazette* in 2016 to become executive director of PublicSource, a nonprofit organization that "presents a bold vision for local journalism in the Pittsburgh region" (PublicSource 2018). In addition, she said she left when she received "a wonderful offer from PublicSource and an opportunity to invent the newsroom on my own terms"

Mila Sanina, former deputy managing editor of the *Post-Gazette,* credited editor David Shribman with keeping the newspaper viable but criticized the racist perspectives of the newspaper's editorial board. (Photo by Mary Lou Nemanic, 2015.)

(Sanina e-mail). Sanina said she has no regrets about leaving, not only because of "the philosophy of the editorial board" but also because of the newsroom shrinkage that will certainly inhibit its public service mission (Sanina interview, March 5, 2018; Sanina e-mail).

Sanina started at the *Post-Gazette* in 2011 as its first social media editor. She then became online engagement editor, assistant managing editor of digital operations, and finally deputy managing editor, the third in the newspaper's management hierarchy. Although the newspaper was initially "a bit slow in accepting the web," by the time she left, she said she felt most of the staff understood the importance of digital journalism (Sanina interview, August 18, 2015). Sanina described her work as deputy managing editor as difficult because, despite the quality journalism produced by its talented staff, the newspaper management's "vision and will to change were not strong enough to offset the difficulty of change" (Sanina interview, March 5, 2018). She said she found it "heartbreaking" to see how buyouts and attrition were gradually shrinking the newsroom as staff members continued to work without a contract. Sanina was particularly concerned about cutbacks in local coverage evident, for example, when the newspaper no longer assigned reporters to regularly cover city council meetings (Sanina interview, March 5, 2018).

Nonetheless Sanina applauded the efforts of Shribman, who she said was protective of the newsroom and was "good at preserving and managing the politics of it" (Sanina interview, March 5, 2018). In terms of experimentation, Sanina, along with several staff members, expressed appreciation for the newspaper's continuing support for experimental projects both online and in print. In particular Sanina highlighted her involvement in the Digs Project, which digitized the newspaper's photo archives relating to historic Pittsburgh. The project team then paired stories on different historic time periods with slideshows and posted them online. Eventually the photos and text were repurposed for the newspaper.

However, Sanina was critical of the newspaper's experimental platform NewsSlide, adopted in 2017. This is an interactive app for tablets and mobile devices that the *Post-Gazette* promoted for its "stunning visuals, photo galleries and videos . . . [e]xclusive stories and special content" that provided the reader with an "immersive, dynamic and intuitive experience" (PG NewsSlide 2019). Sanina said that in addition to being very expensive, the app could be updated only once a day, making it a poor vehicle for breaking news (Sanina interview, March 5, 2018).

Coinciding with the newspaper's reduction to five publishing days was an ad campaign that BCI claimed was intended to encourage readers to use the *Post-Gazette*'s digital platforms, including NewsSlide, post-gazette.com, and PGe, a digital replica of the print version (Deppen 2018a). However, rather than directly promoting its digital products, it concentrated on TV ads and billboards that offensively featured older readers declaring they'll never go digital. One TV ad that some found particularly offensive depicts an older woman sitting on a sofa reading the newspaper saying, "PGe and PG NewsSlide, who the [bleep] needs them. Last time I went online they tried to track my cookies. They'll never get my cookie recipe" (Deppen 2018a).

In an article on a local digital news site, *The Incline,* this campaign was criticized for portraying "older readers as recalcitrant, cranky and technophobic," and the American Association of Retired Persons reported it had received complaints from a few of its members (Deppen 2018a). Andrew Conte, director of Point Park University's Center for Media Innovation, described it as "a bizarre campaign" and speculated that "they must be trying to shock people because on its face it seems unusual to make fun of your customers and do it in a mocking and irreverent way" (quoted in Deppen 2018a). Media analyst Ken Doctor noted that "the problem here is if you're going to flip a switch and move from print to digital, you need to have prepared the path for readers and advertisers. . . . I don't think the *Post-Gazette* gave enough lead time. I'm talking about a process that takes years, not weeks" (quoted in Deppen 2018b).

This push to shift readers to digital platforms foregrounded the racial and economic disparities in Pittsburgh that preclude access to high-speed Internet. According to the city's 2017 equity report, "27.6 percent of black families do not have broadband internet at home compared to only 12.2 percent of white families" (quoted in Deppen 2018b). Brian Cook, president of the Pittsburgh Black Media Federation, explained to *The Incline*, "There is a digital divide, unfortunately. . . . I would hope people who either can't afford it or who don't have access to the internet will utilize local libraries and take a look at the *Post-Gazette* and other media organizations online that way" (quoted in Deppen 2018b).

In addition, in an article on triblive.com, the *Post-Gazette*'s digital-only rival, Fuoco noted, "It's obviously a cost-cutting move, but my understanding is that 80 percent of our revenue still comes from print, so I'm not sure what we gain. . . . I don't know if this is penny-wise and pound-foolish" (quoted in Lindstrom 2018). Fuoco also stressed that the shift away from print had come while contract negotiations had been in limbo for about sixteen months, and the staff had been without raises for about twelve years. "We feel that they are trying to bust the unions," he said (Lindstrom 2018).

Fuoco also expressed concern for the newspaper's public service mission. "I know that it's a difficult time for newspapers, but I think that the Blocks need to also recognize that there's a public trust and a public responsibility that they have by owning a newspaper that's been in existence for 231 years. . . . I would hate to think that they're abandoning that legacy" (quoted in Lindstrom 2018).

Although public service reporting has diminished as the newspaper staff has decreased and multimedia responsibilities have increased, Silver emphasized that in 2018 the newspaper was still fulfilling its public service role with long-term and investigative projects despite their time crunch.

> For people like me and my colleagues at regional papers, who are not functioning at the level of the *New York Times* or the *Washington Post* . . . and who are not on the biggest stage, it is vitally important for us to continue that

> kind of work on the smaller stage. . . . Watchdog journalism is crucial because without that, I really do believe democracy erodes. People get away with things. . . . [I]t's human nature. Absolute power corrupts absolutely. (Silver interview, March 6, 2018)

Silver cited several examples of major public service pieces published by the newspaper, including one on opioid addiction and another on debtor's prisons for people unable to pay court fines and costs. As assignment editor, Silver said it is a pleasure to work with the staff on investigative and innovative projects and that these typically feature impressive visual journalism as well (Silver interview, March 6, 2018).

Visual journalism in these public service projects, as well as on a daily basis in print and online, was also emphasized in staff interviews as a key strength of the *Pittsburgh Post-Gazette.* Its photojournalists, including Stephanie Strasburg, who worked for the *Post-Gazette*'s former competitor, the *Tribune-Review,* before Shribman recruited her in 2016, have won international and national awards. Strasburg said she appreciates management's openness to innovative story ideas and the fact that they realize they have to think outside the box. One example she cited was a project she developed in 2018 while covering the opioid crisis. This involved working with a little girl caught in the middle of the crisis who photographed her own story as she created her own alphabet (Strasburg interview).

The *Post-Gazette*'s openness to staff-generated story ideas was echoed by Julia Rendleman, a staff photojournalist hired in 2012, who left to freelance in 2016 (Rendleman interview, June 7, 2018). She highlighted a 2014 project on the Pittsburgh Marathon in which she rode on a bike and took photos of the event along the route to give readers an "inside" perspective (Rendleman interview, August 18, 2015). The newspaper even set up an online page dedicated to Rendleman's coverage so that readers could follow her in real time.

Overall, as the *Pittsburgh Post-Gazette* has continued to experiment with online delivery, sometimes unsuccessfully by misjudging older readers, it has still been successful in attracting more readers annually. In addition, it has thus far maintained its commitment to investigative and visual reportage. Nonetheless, besides the challenges of developing multiplatform delivery, the newspaper still faces ongoing challenges with labor negotiations, journalistic autonomy, and editorial accountability that overshadow its continuing viability.

Conclusion

The challenges facing these Rust Belt newspapers shine light on the crisis in the newspaper industry and its evolution to multiplatform delivery. Both the *Pittsburgh Post-Gazette* and the *Buffalo News* have survived because of their many loyal readers and because their owners are committed to supporting newspapers. Despite Pittsburgh's nuanced and gradual transition into multiplatform delivery and its robust newsroom numbers, the newspaper faces major challenges in labor negotiations, in understanding seniors and low-income readers, and in the areas of journalistic and editorial autonomy. In Buffalo the major challenges involve multiplatform delivery with a bare-bones staff and adaptation to Digital First at the expense of the newspaper. At this point, the only outcomes that can be foreseen with certainty are that the multiplatform transitions for these two Rust Belt metros will be ongoing and that work practices will continue to evolve along with technology. As Chapter 5 shows, similar challenges can be seen in the Twin Cities of Minnesota, an area that is unique because its two metro dailies cover a single metropolitan market.

5

The *St. Paul Pioneer Press* and the *Minneapolis Star Tribune*

Two Metros in One Market

This chapter examines the unique problems newspapers face under hedge fund ownership. Known by their critics as vulture capitalists, these owners continue to squeeze profits from newsrooms across the country by stripping their staffs to the bare bones. Instead of reinvesting newspaper profits back into their newspapers, the companies typically divert profits to other businesses. What is at stake is the elimination of original local reporting, the heart of the public service roles that newspapers have historically filled. Specifically, this chapter examines the decimation of metro daily newsrooms through the lenses of two Minnesota newspapers, the *St. Paul Pioneer Press* and the *Minneapolis Star Tribune,* which were once embroiled in a fierce rivalry to serve the Minneapolis–St. Paul metro area. Although this area, known as the Twin Cities, is considered a single commercial market, it consists of two very distinctive cities that in 2018 comprised a population of more than 3.6 million (*World Population Review* 2018). The following case studies foreground how ownership and operational policies impact the viability of metro dailies.

Although historically both the *Pioneer Press* and the *Star Tribune* have had multiple owners and both have been owned by private equity firms, the *Star Tribune* staff interviewed for this book considered the newspaper fortunate to have been purchased by a local investment company after bankruptcy and then by a civic benefactor in 2014. In contrast, the *St. Paul Pioneer Press* has been owned since 2012 by Digital First Media, whose parent company, Alden Global Capital, has a reputation for its profiteering practices, which in 2017 yielded a profit margin of 17 percent (Doctor 2018; NewsGuild 2018). This is well above the profit margins of most media companies, which averaged less than 10 percent in that year (Doctor 2018). In 2018 layoffs and buyouts under Alden's ownership reduced the *Pioneer Press*'s staff to fewer than 50 from a peak of about 260 in the late 1990s (Orrick interview, April 26, 2018). In fact, just during the course of this study, the newsroom was cut by more than half in only three years—from about 95 in 2015 to 46 in 2018 (Westpfahl interviews, May 18, 2015, and April 3, 2018; Orrick interview, April 26, 2018).

In 2018 the *Star Tribune* was thriving, but this has not always been the case. The newspaper went through bankruptcy in 2009 after a steep decline in advertising and under the burden of a huge debt load from its acquisition by a New York–based hedge fund (Fitzgerald 2009). Less than a year after declaring bankruptcy, the paper emerged financially stable, and was eventually purchased by a local partnership, which was acquired in 2014 by a civic benefactor.

Different Cities with a Single Metro Area

Minneapolis and St. Paul have a rich media landscape with both traditional and digital media. These towns are known as the Twin Cities because they border each other and form one large metropolitan area asymmetrically divided by the Mississippi River. But these cities are hardly twins. Topographically they really do not look that much alike, nor do they have the same populations—St. Paul, the state capital, has just over 300,000 people and Minneapolis has more than 420,000 (*World Population Review* 2018). As both cities developed, Minneapolis became known for flour and lumber milling and St. Paul as a hub for transportation and trade (Atkins 2018). Minneapolis, the younger of the two cities, is known for its progressive ethos, its downtown skyline dotted with modern skyscrapers that mark its centrality in business and finance. In contrast, St. Paul, with a smaller downtown district and a more casual atmosphere, is known for its historic preservation of many old buildings and for its many close-knit neighborhoods surrounding the downtown area.

Besides their economic differences, these cities have cultural distinctions that are quite pronounced. In fact, some natives use an alcoholic metaphor to describe the different characters of these two cities, branding Minneapolis "a champagne town, [and] St. Paul a shot and a beer" (Wingerd 2007). And, almost from their inceptions, a rivalry developed between these two towns.

This is exemplified by what were called the Census Wars of 1890, as the population of Minneapolis threatened to surpass that of the older city, St. Paul. Accounts of the wars depict census takers fabricating names and addresses to inflate each city's numbers and arrests of census takers for fraudulent activities (Klein 2017). Over the years this rivalry grew so intense that one historical account highlights a 1930s article in *Fortune* magazine in which "the most important fact to know about the Twin Cities was that 'they hate each other'" (quoted in Wingerd 2007).

Early Newspapers in the Twin Cities

As the Twin Cities population grew, so did a bustling newspaper scene. The first paper, a capital city weekly known as the *Minnesota Pioneer,* began printing in 1849 in St. Paul (C. Sterling 2009). By 1855 five dailies were established there. Over the rest of the nineteenth and into the twentieth century, St. Paul dailies competed with not only each other but also the dailies established in its sister city, Minneapolis.

The *Pioneer Press* can be traced back to the *Minnesota Pioneer* and the *Saint Paul Dispatch* (C. Sterling 2009). In 1927 both papers were acquired by Ridder Publications and operated separately as morning and afternoon newspapers until 1985, when they were merged into an all-day newspaper, the *St. Paul Pioneer Press and Dispatch.* In 1990 "Dispatch" was dropped from its title and the newspaper became a morning-only daily. In 2012 Digital First Media, owned by Alden Global Capital, bought the *Pioneer Press.*

Minneapolis's first weekly started in 1851, but the city had no daily newspaper until 1867, when the *Minneapolis Tribune* was established. The *Minneapolis Tribune*'s primary competition within the city became the *Minneapolis Daily Star,* established in 1920. These competing newspapers were consolidated during the 1930s and 1940s, with the *Tribune* as a morning paper and the *Star* as an evening paper. In 1982 the two merged under the name the *Star Tribune* (C. Sterling 2009).

Despite its annual advertising and circulation declines typical of many other metros at the time, the *Star Tribune*'s newsroom peaked in the late 1990s at around 450 employees. In the twenty-first century, after a turbulent period during which the newspaper was sold and resold, it was purchased in 2007 by a New York–based hedge fund, Avista Capital Partners (Fitzgerald 2009; Phelps 2009). As the recession accelerated advertising declines, Avista reduced the number of pages in the *Star Tribune,* cut its staff down to about 260, and cut back on other expenses. However, although still profitable and ranked as the fifteenth-largest newspaper in the United States, the *Star Tribune* did not create enough profitability to cover the debt load of its hedge fund owner; consequently, in 2009 the newspaper filed for Chapter 11 bankruptcy protection (Fitzgerald 2009; Edmonds 2016b; Doctor 2013a). In less than a year the *Star Tribune* had stabilized and emerged from bankruptcy. In 2012 the newspaper was purchased by locally owned equity fund Wayzata Investment Partners, a company that was bought in 2014 by billionaire businessman Glen Taylor, also owner of the professional basketball team the Minnesota Timberwolves (Edmonds 2016b; Doctor 2013b). Since its bankruptcy the newsroom has held steady at about 260 staff members and is considered "fully staffed" (Kelly interview).

Newspaper Rivalry

For most of their histories, the scrappy, smaller *St. Paul Pioneer Press* competed with the bigger city's Goliath, the *Minneapolis*

Star Tribune, over the same metropolitan area. During the late twentieth century their scoops were a source of civic pride, an extension of loyalties for residents' respective cities.

By the last half of the twentieth century, the antipathy between the cities had begun to subside with the establishment of such joint efforts as the Minneapolis–St. Paul International Airport, the Minnesota Twins professional baseball team, and the Metropolitan Council, which oversees the seven-county metropolitan area. By the beginning of the twenty-first century, the rivalry between the two newspapers had also subsided, as newsroom cuts contracted the *Pioneer Press*'s coverage area to St. Paul, especially focusing on the city's East Metro area (Westpfahl interview, April 3, 2018; Webster interview; Orrick interview, April 26, 2018). Yet vestiges of the rivalry were still evident in 2018, as core readers remained loyal to the *Pioneer Press* even as the subscription rates increased and the newspaper became smaller, with fewer stories and less original reporting. According to former deputy managing editor for digital and social media Jennifer Westpfahl, "St. Paul people are not going to read the *Star Tribune,* and Minneapolis people are not going to read the *Pioneer Press*" (Westpfahl interview, April 3, 2018).

Dave Orrick, state government and politics reporter for the *St. Paul Pioneer Press,* noted that, despite being more subdued, in 2018 the "rivalry still exists in certain areas such as sports and politics," but it had certainly diminished compared to past years (Orrick interview, April 26, 2018). Jim Gehrz, freelance photographer formerly with the *Star Tribune* and the *Pioneer Press,* said he missed the competition between the two papers: "It was not always fun, but it was healthy" for both newspapers (Gehrz interview, March 25, 2013).

Hedge Fund Ownership: Alden/Digital First Media

Since 2016, Julie Reynolds, a freelance reporter and former reporter for a Digital First Media (DFM) newspaper, has been investigating the business practices of DFM, the second-largest newspaper chain in America, for #NewsMatters, a website for DFM workers sponsored by NewsGuild–Communications Workers of America. This site is part of a "national, coordinated campaign to win fair contracts with wage increases for the nearly 1,000 Guild-represented employees of Digital First Media" (DFM Workers 2018). Reynolds's work, and that of a few other investigative journalists, has focused on how the profiteering practices of hedge funds have accelerated the decline of the newspaper industry: "I think in 2018 the narrative is changing. People are no longer buying the story that the Internet killed newspapers and that's the only reason all this is happening. I think they finally realize there's something else at work and that something is hedge funds" (quoted in Hutchins 2018).

Reynolds and several media analysts have increasingly underscored the divergent missions of hedge funds and newspapers (Doctor 2018; Mullen 2016a). Hedge funds are privately owned companies that typically buy distressed or declining properties and strip them for profits before finally selling off their remains. And, since 2012, the *Pioneer Press* has been owned by DFM, whose parent company is the hedge fund Alden Global Capital.

Washington Post media critic Margaret Sullivan described Alden as "one of the most ruthless corporate strip-miners seemingly intent on destroying local journalism" (2018b). That is because it has been shrinking the staffs of its newspaper properties at "twice the industry average" (NewsGuild 2018). According to media analyst Ken Doctor, these cutbacks allowed it to operate at a 17 percent profit margin on profits of $159 million in 2017, at a time when other major media publishers, including Gannett and the New York Times Company, operated on margins of less than 10 percent (Doctor 2018). Consequently, it was clear to Doctor "that Alden has transformed Digital First Media into a non-stop cash register" (Doctor 2018). Doctor's financial revelations were particularly shocking to the remaining staff of the *Pioneer Press*, who learned that their paper made $10 million in profits in 2017—providing DFM with a 13 percent profit margin—while the newspaper's staff had been cut to under fifty (Doctor 2018).

A lawsuit filed in March 2018 by the minority shareholder of DFM, another hedge fund called Solus Alternative Asset Management, also highlighted Alden's profiteering practices. The lawsuit charges that Alden created a "purposefully obfuscated" subsidiary, Twenty Lake Holdings, and "siphoned hundreds of millions of dollars from one of America's largest news chains[,] . . . damaging local news organizations to finance insider investment deals" (Reynolds 2018b). One of these risky non-newspaper investments included a failing pharmacy chain. The lawsuit "also describes an insider 'sale/leaseback' in which Twenty Lake apparently bought a property from DFM-Alden and then leased it back to the news chain" (Reynolds 2018b).

While some journalists at DFM newspapers have called Alden "horrible and evil" for its profiteering practices, Orrick is less judgmental, underscoring the fact that newspapers and hedge funds have very different missions (Orrick interview, April 26, 2018). He explained that hedge funds are set up solely to make profits, without regard for the quality of the newspapers or for the public service interests they represent, while the mission of newspapers is to provide an essential public service while also making a profit.

In 2014, as the staff count in the *Pioneer Press*'s newsroom began to dip below one hundred, Orrick, who is a representative of the Minnesota Newspaper and Communications Guild, became concerned about the viability of his newspaper, and got involved in a guild-sponsored advertising campaign in which several DFM newspapers placed ads in their respective newspapers calling for new ownership. Although the *Pioneer Press* refused to publish the ad, it appeared in the *Minneapolis Star Tribune* (Minnesota News Guild 2014):

> Dear Newspaper Readers,
>
> For more than 150 years, the *St. Paul Pioneer* Press has been an essential source of news and advertising for the Twin Cities, providing unmatched coverage of St. Paul and the east metro area. That coverage is now at risk. Unfortunately, the newspaper's current owner, New York City–

The owners of the *St. Paul Pioneer Press* sold the newspaper's downtown building and relocated to a leased space just outside the city center. (Photo by Mary Lou Nemanic, 2016.)

> based hedge fund Alden Global Capital, is more interested in dismantling the newspaper to increase profits than in investing in the future. The Twin Cities deserve better. The *Pioneer Press* needs a new owner who cares about the community it serves and will be a responsible steward of Minnesota's oldest news organization. All serious, interested parties should contact the Minnesota Newspaper and Communications Guild at 612-789-0044.
>
> Sincerely,
> The Minnesota Newspaper and
> Communications Guild

Adding to Orrick's concern for the newspaper's viability was the sale of the newspaper's building and printing plant, estimated to be worth more than $4 million and more than $2 million, respectively, with "virtually none of the profit" reinvested in the *Pioneer Press* (Orrick interview, April 26, 2018). According to Julie Reynolds, Alden's pattern of selling newspaper buildings is particularly problematic: "If you had a building and you had land, it meant during hard times you could get a line of credit and survive a recession. . . . That was the security blanket that was ripped out from under these papers. . . . [T]hat just means these people are not planning on us having a future" (quoted in Hutchins 2018).

In 2018, as journalists at DFM newspapers witnessed their buildings being sold and their newsrooms gutted, the website dfmworkers.org became an increasingly prominent hub for the mobilization of journalists/activists attempting to save their newspapers from Alden's destructive ownership in what analysts called "an open rebellion" (NewsGuild 2018; DFM Workers 2018). Their mobilization efforts accelerated after the buyouts of about one-third of *Denver Post* newsroom staff and the paper's publication of a six-page editorial section that condemned Alden's profiteering practices and demanded new ownership. The editorials attracted international media attention and alerted the public about the newspaper's decline at the hands of the "vulture capitalist" owners (NewsGuild 2018).

One of the most prominent mobilization efforts was a demonstration in front of Alden's New York headquarters in May 2018, shortly after the *Denver Post* buyouts. This event drew journalists from several DFM newspapers across the United States, including representatives from the *Pioneer Press.* United under the slogan—"invest or sell"—demonstrators "picketed, chanted and gave speeches on bullhorns. They demanded that Alden invest in the papers it owns or sell them to someone who will" (NewsGuild 2018). When the protestors tried to present Alden with petitions signed by journalists from their newspapers, the company's security officers refused to allow them into the company's headquarters or to accept their petitions on behalf of Alden (NewsGuild 2018). This rebellion of DFM journalists eventually led to censorship efforts by Alden, in the form of directives to their newspapers to remove negative references to Alden or DFM in any local or wire service content (Reynolds 2018a). Prior to this time, DFM had been typically disengaged with the editorial operations of its newspapers (Reynolds 2018a).

Despite the efforts of both the *Pioneer Press* and the *Denver Post,* finding a new owner and convincing Alden to sell is expected to be an uphill battle, given the high rate of return the company gains from harvesting these newspapers (Doctor 2018). An additional disadvantage for the *Pioneer Press* is its market overlap with the very successful *Star Tribune* (Doctor 2018).

Literature on Quality Journalism and Profitability

DFM's newspaper staffs are not alone in their concern for the viability of newspapers under hedge fund ownership. Studies conducted by Philip Meyer and by Stephen Lacy, Michael Stamm, and Hugh Martin have revealed a strong correlation between divestment in print operations and a decline in the quality of the print product that eventually leads to decreases in advertising revenue and circulation numbers (Lacy, Stamm, and Martin 2014; Meyer 2009). Harvesting strategies employed by companies such as Alden profitably strip a declining business of its assets through layoffs, buyouts, wage reductions, furloughs, cutbacks in coverage areas, and reductions in the size of newspapers as well as cutbacks in newsroom resources (Starkman 2014; Lacy, Stamm, and Martin 2014; Waldman 2011; Meyer 2009).

Reynolds, a freelance writer who had worked previously at the DFM paper the *Monterey Herald,* told the *Columbia Journalism Review* that the cutbacks in resources at the paper were so extreme "it got to the point where literally you couldn't get a manila folder, you had to buy your own pens. There was no hot water to wash your hands in the building" (quoted in Hutchins 2018). Doctor also noted that "at DFM's suburban Philadelphia dailies, located in affluent markets, the daily concerns are both big picture and more mundane: rats, mildew, falling ceilings.... Those Philly suburbans—rats, mildew and all—lead the whole company in profit margin, at a whopping 30 percent" (Doctor 2018).

Meyer's book, *The Vanishing Newspaper,* describes the impact of harvesting on the newspaper industry:

> A stagnant industry's market position is harvested by raising prices and lowering quality, trusting that the customers will continue to be attracted by the brand name rather than the substance for which the brand once stood. Eventually, of course, they will wake up. But, as the harvest metaphor implies, this is a nonrenewable, take-the-money-and-run strategy. A given crop can only be harvested once. (2009, 14)

Orrick noted that the *Pioneer Press*'s extremely loyal readership would appeal to a harvesting company like Alden:

> There's a real lag between when the paper no longer becomes good to somebody and when the money stops rolling in. . . . Tomorrow they could basically lay off the entire newsroom and just run some AP stories and some AP photos in the paper and it would probably take six months before the legions of people realized—"Oh, my God, this is not worth a dime; this doesn't cover any local news any more"—before they would actually cancel subscriptions and that cash flow would stop coming in. Alden has been banking on that, which makes total business sense for them. The thing that I've been telling people is hedge funds and local newspapers are just a bad match. They're just not compatible. You have a group of investors . . . who want a rate of return that is unsustainable from the product that we have right now . . . and our mission is not to be a cash flow operation. . . . [O]ur mission is to serve our community and the public. (Orrick interview, April 26, 2018)

The *Pioneer Press:* Struggling to Stay Alive

The *Pioneer Press* has had a reputation for excellent journalism, especially in its legislative coverage. The newspaper has won national and international awards, including three Pulitzer Prizes:

Dedicated to her job, Jennifer Westpfahl, former deputy editor at the *Pioneer Press,* nevertheless felt compelled to leave the newspaper when the decimation of the newsroom became too stressful. (Photo by Mary Lou Nemanic, 2016.)

in 1986, 1988, and 2000 (C. Sterling 2009; Orrick interview, April 26, 2018). In 2016, when the newsroom still had around seventy to seventy-five journalists, an article highlighting Orrick's search for a locally based owner dismally depicted the paper's status: "The oldest newspaper in Minnesota had been reduced to a skeleton. Now its overlords were simply picking at the bones" (Mullen 2016a). Remarkably, two years later, the *Pioneer Press* was still putting out a newspaper with only forty-six people on staff. Despite the cuts that have been "brutal on morale," Orrick said that he believed that the remaining staff "are there because they love it. They're true believers. . . . The *Pioneer Press* is still a fun place to work" (Orrick interview, April 26, 2018).

One of those true believers, Westpfahl, hung on until early 2018, finding it very difficult to leave despite a very good job offer from a Minneapolis public relations and marketing firm. She had spent about a decade at the *Pioneer Press,* starting as a copyeditor in 2006. She was laid off in 2009, but was rehired in 2011 as a Web producer and was eventually promoted to deputy editor for digital news and social media. By the time she left, her job had become "way too stressful," as she witnessed the decimation of the newsroom and had to cope with the depleted staff morale:

> I couldn't take it anymore—people coming to me day after day saying: "I can't do my job; I don't have enough hours in the day; I don't have the updated technology; we don't have the resources we need; we don't have leadership that understands what we should be doing" . . . and there was nothing I could do for them. (Westpfahl interview, April 3, 2018)

Although Westpfahl said she has not regretted her decision to leave, her attachment to the newspaper was still evident throughout a 2018 interview in which she made several comments about the newspaper as if she were still on staff. She even caught herself once: "Notice I still say 'we'" (Westpfahl interview, April 3, 2018). This dedication to the paper was also evident in her description of its strengths:

> The people there are fabulous, I would hire most of them any day. They are really committed to what they are doing; otherwise they probably wouldn't still be there because you really have to be committed to weather this. . . . The culture of the organization has always been the smaller, scrappy underdog to the *Star Tribune*. So it has always been a very bottom-up place, empowering employees to come up with their own story ideas. . . . The *Star Tribune*, I have heard, is very top-down . . . and if you wanted to come up with something, you'd have to go through six layers of approval. And the *Pioneer Press* is very like: "Hey, I had an idea." . . . "Okay, go do it." They are very nimble, and their employees are very empowered to try new things. (Westpfahl interview, April 3, 2018)

This description of a more formal, structured ethos at the *Star Tribune* was confirmed by Colleen Kelly, senior digital editor at the *Star Tribune.* Kelly had previously worked at the *Pioneer Press,* and also described it as a "bottom-up operation" (Kelly interview).

The *Pioneer Press*'s connection to the city of St. Paul was another major strength Westpfahl identified. "No one else is as invested in St. Paul the way we are," she said (Westpfahl interview, April 3, 2018). In addition, she pointed out that the *Pioneer Press* was fully committed to a multiplatform approach that she called "Digital Right." This means that "sometimes it's right for it [content] to be first on digital and sometimes it's right to be first in the paper" (Westpfahl 2018). Digital Right also means determining separate deadlines for publishing stories in print and on the different digital platforms, including the website, social media, and newsletters.

To illustrate the differences between the Digital-First approach and the Digital-Right approach, Westpfahl cited the example of a story scheduled to appear in print on a Sunday. With Digital First, the story would have to appear online by Saturday. In contrast with Digital Right—because online audiences are typically small on Saturdays—the story might instead appear online on Thursday or Friday or might even be held till Monday or Tuesday because those are high traffic times for the website (Westpfahl interview, April 3, 2018).

Even though Digital Right takes a multiplatform approach, Westpfahl noted that the *Pioneer Press*'s website, twincities.com, was limited to still photography that includes photo galleries and slideshows. It typically does not include videos because these are not popular with their readers and they are too time-consuming to produce with a shrinking newsroom staff (Westpfahl interview, April 3, 2018).

Orrick emphasized that another major strength of the *Pioneer Press,* and a continuing area of competition with the *Star Tribune,* is its capitol coverage, even though the *Star Tribune* has five reporters covering the legislature while the *Pioneer Press*

Despite the drastic reduction in the newsroom staff at the *Pioneer Press*, Dave Orrick, who covers state government and politics, still considers the newspaper a fun place to work. (Photo by Mary Lou Nemanic, 2015.)

has two (Orrick interview, April 26, 2018). Orrick is one of those reporters. He joined the newspaper in 2006 as a general assignment reporter and in 2008 was assigned the St. Paul city hall beat (Orrick interview, May 18, 2015). In 2011 he was offered his "dream job" as outdoors editor—editing, writing, and photographing for the paper's Outdoors section in the "Land of 10,000 Lakes." But in 2016 staff cuts led to the elimination of the outdoors beat, so Orrick took a position on the Web desk for a year, after which he volunteered to cover the state government and politics beat when a position opened up (Orrick interview, April 26, 2018).

Challenges at the *Pioneer Press*

In 2018 Orrick said the *Pioneer Press*'s biggest challenge was finding an owner who cares about quality local journalism (Orrick interview, April 26, 2018). Yet despite the newspaper's declining staff, he remained positive in his tireless efforts to find a local owner: "We are modern, digital journalists running a newsroom that kicks as much butt as we can for a company that's making a profit in a difficult market. We want people interested in buying us to realize that" (quoted in Uren 2018). Although this is a slow process, and Orrick was not at liberty to divulge any details, he said he's made "good progress" in conversations with potential buyers and has considered different ownership models, including nonprofit (Orrick interview, April 26, 2018; Uren 2018).

Although the *Pioneer Press* perseveres, staff members emphasize that the cuts have taken their toll not only in terms of a coverage area that excludes Minneapolis and the reduced size of the newspaper but also a decrease in the variety of stories once routinely published. Of particular concern were the newspaper's health and business beats. Orrick also expressed concern about the decimation of the copy desk, the reduction of the photo staff to two full-time and one half-time photojournalists, and the virtual elimination of long-form and investigative reporting (Orrick interview, April 26, 2018). The lack of an investigative reporting team was particularly disturbing to Orrick, and he cited an example that occurred in 2017 when the *Pioneer Press* broke a story on elder abuse in nursing homes. Because the newspaper no longer had a large enough staff to do investigative follow-ups, the *Star Tribune* was able to steal their thunder and develop the story into "a full exposé" online, complete with photo layouts and videos. The online series won several public service awards from organizations such as the Society of Professional Journalists and the Associated Press Media Editors (Orrick interview, April 26, 2018).

Only time will tell if the *Pioneer Press* can find new ownership to rebuild its newsroom after such a brutal harvesting. Analysts have said they are baffled that in a big city like St. Paul local leaders have not stepped up to save the newspaper when it is so valuable in terms of public service (Collins 2016; Mullen 2016b). As Orrick wistfully observed in *City Pages*, a publication owned by the *Star Tribune*: "We're the Twin Cities, and each city deserves its own paper. . . . In a perfect world, Glen Taylor would have a twin brother who could buy the *Pioneer Press* to protect it from the continued cuts our hedge fund owner is demanding" (Mullen 2016b).

Minneapolis Star Tribune: From Survival to Success

Although it is rare for a newspaper to receive a Pulitzer Prize, and it is even less likely for a newspaper to receive more than one Pulitzer Prize in a single year, the *Minneapolis Star Tribune* won two in 2013. Remarkably, these came only four years after declaring bankruptcy (Edmonds 2016b; Doctor 2013b). One of the prizes, for a series on infant day-care deaths, recognized the newspaper's outstanding work in investigative journalism. The series' publication resulted in a dramatic drop in day-care deaths and legislative reform of Minnesota's day-care regulations (Meryhew 2013). The *Star Tribune*'s other Pulitzer Prize recognized the body of work of editorial cartoonist Steve Sack. Sack joined the *Star Tribune* in 1981 and was a Pulitzer Prize finalist in 2004.

The *Star Tribune* is distributed throughout the Twin Cities metropolitan area, the state of Minnesota, and the Upper Midwest. The paper and its predecessors have won a total of six Pulitzer Prizes. In 2016 the Nielsen Scarborough Multi-Market Studies ranked the *Star Tribune* No. 1 nationally in daily and in Sunday readership (Hare 2016). In recent years, it has received international accolades as a successful model for regional dailies (Edmonds 2016b). In 2012, only three years after bankruptcy, this newspaper was described in the *American Journalism Review* as

> one of the fine regional newspapers in the country. From the front page through all of the section fronts, the paper captures a true sense of living in a smart, connected city in one of the northernmost and mostly rural parts of America. Big ticket investigations read like answers to real community problems rather than responses to a call for prize-contending ideas in an editorial meeting. Eight- and 12-inch stories show an attention to detail. The *Star Tribune* is worth paying for. (Lisheron 2012)

The *Star Tribune* not only publishes quality content; it even makes a small profit for its owner, billionaire Glen Taylor (Edmonds 2016b). Nonetheless, many staff members recalled the difficult days before the bankruptcy, when the newspaper was owned by its first hedge fund, Avista (*Star-Tribune* interviews, 2015–2018). Back in 2007 and 2008, despite its profitability, the *Star Tribune* was struggling because its profits did not amount to enough to cover Avista's debt to acquire the newspaper (Fitzgerald 2009). Initially Avista tried to cut costs by furloughs, layoffs, buyouts, and attrition—shaving down the staff of about 400 to about 250 (Hare 2016; Lisheron 2012). The number of pages in the newspaper was reduced, along with other operating expenses, but these cuts were not enough (Lisheron 2012). Under bankruptcy protection, the *Star Tribune* restructured its finances and eliminated a large portion of its debt by selling its building and five blocks of downtown property worth approximately $38.5 million (Belz 2014). Emerging from bankruptcy, the *Star Tribune* was then bought by a more benign local hedge fund that was purchased by local billionaire Glen Taylor in 2014. In an article on the selling and reselling of the *Star Tribune,* the authors note that the bumpy road had prepared the newspaper for better times: "In a sense, two rounds of private equity owners and a bankruptcy did the dirty work of ruthlessly cutting costs, laying off employees, and re-negotiating union contracts, allowing a benign local owner to acquire the paper at a sustainable price" (Kuttner and Zenger 2017).

While Taylor admitted purchasing the newspaper was a good investment, he wrote that he also bought the paper because, since his youth on a farm in southern Minnesota, the *Star Tribune* had provided "Minnesota's window on the larger world."

> My heart belongs to Minnesota—and Minnesota deserves a news organization of the caliber of the *Star Tribune*. . . . I'm drawn to things that unite all Minnesotans. . . . I see the *Star Tribune* as a force for bringing Minnesotans together. . . . Minnesotans have long turned to the *Star Tribune* as the most authoritative source of information

The new newsroom of the *Minneapolis Star Tribune* is designed to emphasize multimedia and 24/7 online news deadlines. (Photo by Mary Lou Nemanic, 2015.)

> they need to be good citizens. I aim to keep that trust. (Taylor 2014)

Staff members generally commended Taylor for his pledge to allow the paper free rein to operate as usual, which he announced to the staff: "I'm not going to be hands on in the sense that I run the paper. But I am going to be hands on in the sense if you guys need some capital or something new. I am going to be hands on if you guys are looking at some technology that I am [already] working on over here. We can work together" (quoted in Robson 2014).

As the newspaper prospered under Taylor's ownership, its 2015 move to a new space provided an opportunity to restructure the paper's production practices along with its physical configuration. According to Jenni Pinkley, senior video editor, the custom design of this newsroom reflects the paper's increasing multimedia emphasis and the 24/7 deadlines of its website (Pinkley interview). The new *Star Tribune* newsroom is centrally located in downtown Minneapolis on the thirteenth floor of an office tower with windows overlooking stunning views of the downtown and surrounding area. A multimedia news hub or "command center" for breaking news is in the middle of the newsroom, along with a circular kiosk of televisions constantly broadcasting a variety of news channels (Painter 2015). The newsroom also reflects a substantial investment in video and photo studios and in private and collaborative work spaces (Painter 2015).

According to its publisher and CEO, Mike Klingensmith, a major factor in the *Star Tribune*'s revitalization has been its integrated multiplatform approach that strikes a balance between print and digital platforms (Lisheron 2012; Edmonds 2016b; Bjorhus interview; Kelly interview; Webster interview). In a 2017 article, Klingensmith explained: "We've continued to invest aggressively in print[,] . . . maintaining the newsroom and introducing new sections. We've not cut back on our news well. That has helped us maintain readership while we increase digital income" (quoted in Kuttner and Zenger 2017). Suki Dardarian, senior managing editor and vice president, told the Poynter Institute that because a substantial portion of their audience still reads the newspaper, "print is still critically important"; consequently, they have established an "audience-first" strategy (Hare 2016). In an *American Journalism Review* article, Doctor credited Klingensmith with "looking at the endgame. The print component, the digital, the development of new digital products are all pieces of the revenue puzzle. . . . By being rational, Mike Klingensmith is ahead of the pack" (quoted in Lisheron 2012).

Generally, staff members emphasized that the newspaper's website, startribune.com, is constantly evolving (Kelly interview). Unlike many metro daily websites, including the twincities.com website of the *Pioneer Press*, the *Star Tribune*'s site is not restricted to local news. It maintains a mix of international, national, regional, and local news because it is managed by a news editor and is updated "almost minute by minute" (Kelly interview). Kelly noted that because of this comprehensive array of content on their website, it is "on par with the national news sites" (Kelly interview).

Also exceptional about this newspaper is the fact that "in contrast to many metros across the country, the *Minneapolis*

Star Tribune is home to a uniquely robust newsroom" of around 250 (Hare 2016). Because the newsroom is "fully staffed," investigative and long-form/public service projects can continue to be major features of the newspaper (Kelly interview). In fact, Kelly says, "we have a massive print staff. . . . [A]ctually, it stuns me sometimes" (Kelly interview). Also remarkable is the fact that the *Star Tribune*'s staff includes twenty new hires, mostly in digital positions, who joined the newsroom since 2015 (Hare 2016). As Klingensmith explained to the *American Journalism Review*, in order to produce a quality news product, "the newsroom has to be the last place we go for cost savings. . . . I'm very mindful, really motivated to get employees to feel good about where they work and where we're going" (quoted in Lisheron 2012).

Experimentation and Newsroom Realignment

Staff interviews identified another major factor contributing to the prosperity of the *Star Tribune* as its willingness to experiment with new practices and new ways of telling stories (*Star Tribune* interviews, 2015–2018). Part of this experimental ethos included the paper's involvement with the Knight-Temple Table Stakes Project. Table Stakes is a nonprofit initiative of the John S. and James L. Knight Foundation, Temple University, and the American Press Institute that gives newspapers an opportunity to develop digital best practices, increase digital subscriptions, and improve their community engagement (Knight Foundation 2017). MaryJo Webster, computer-assisted reporting editor, credited Table Stakes with helping "to jump-start things" and with inspiring the "focused hiring and (newsroom) realignment" (Webster interview). Focused hiring for specific multimedia positions was part of the newsroom's realignment, which developed some new teams while retaining a few individual beats. The Quick Strike Team is particularly significant because it is dedicated to fast-breaking news, posting frequent updates of brief stories on the website and social media platforms to keep readers up-to-date. The Quick Strike Team gives other teams and reporters time to produce in-depth and analytical multimedia content for all of the newspaper's platforms (Webster interview; Kelly interview; Hare 2016). Kelly also highlighted the role of Table Stakes in moving the newspaper to earlier online deadlines to accommodate high traffic times and in rescheduling some of its Quick Strike Team to cover those earlier deadlines (Kelly interview).

A good example of the *Star Tribune*'s multiplatform approach involved its 2016 coverage after the sudden death of rock icon Prince. Within minutes, the paper's Quick Strike Team rapidly posted stories online, updating them frequently as the paper's website spiked from an average of 800,000 hits per day to 1.5 million (Edmonds 2016b). Other teams and individuals followed up with postings of a live blog, a timeline, a discography, photo galleries, and videos (Webster interview; Kelly interview; Hare 2017a). Along with new stories written for print editions, much of the online content on Prince was repurposed for the daily newspaper. The newspaper also published a special sixteen-page commemorative section in its Sunday edition (Webster interview; Edmonds 2016b). According to Dardarian, "We did right by digital, which gave us the opportunity to do right by print . . . and we were able to see the magic of that" (quoted in Hare 2016).

Yet even before the newspaper's involvement with Table Stakes, the experimentation ethos of the *Star Tribune* was apparent (Gyllenhaal and Moses 2006). In 2005 the newspaper redesigned its website after conducting numerous reader focus groups and reader interest surveys. As part of the *Star Tribune*'s transition to multiplatform delivery, a centrally located print and online news desk was established in its old newsroom. "We work hard at being truly experimental," Webster stated (Webster interview).

In 2015, after working at *USA Today*, Webster was hired by the *Star Tribune* to work in data journalism. She pointed out that since 2016 the newspaper has made "huge leaps" in the quality and quantity of its content. As data editor, Webster has been involved in numerous public service projects that visualize statistical data through graphs and interactive maps. Interactive maps are particularly useful tools for giving "readers the opportunity to find their own story" and "explore what's meaningful to them" (Webster interview). Webster highlighted an example of an interactive map utilized in land-use stories that allowed readers to compare historical and present-day sites. In another example, the newspaper created an interactive map to locate where citizens had been killed by police, along with biographical data related to each incident. Webster also highlighted the *Star Tribune*'s experimentation with its "Data Drop." This is an online feature that allows the staff to post detailed data from data-rich stories to supplement the publication of online stories. This has been particularly useful for stories on "schools that beat the odds," a popular print feature that the newspaper moved to its digital platform (Webster interview).

Flexibility in writing styles is another area of experimentation at the *Star Tribune* (Kelly interview). Although iterative writing, or online stories in-progress that are updated as they develop, is a common style for breaking news, not all online stories appear in this form. Kelly noted that the newspaper's style is flexible enough that at times print stories are posted online without being repurposed into the more casual, informal style commonly used for the Web (Kelly interview).

The *Star Tribune*'s photojournalism is also a major success factor. Dave Denney, assigning editor and photo editor who joined the staff in 1993, stated the photo staff has been fortunate not to have undergone the cuts so many other metros have endured (Denney interview). With the news organization having thirteen still photographers, all of whom can shoot video; three videographers; five photo editors; and a director of photography, Denney said the staff has time to cover both breaking news and long-term projects. "We have the time we need to spend on assignments. . . . [W]e're really in a good place here" (Denney interview). The *Star Tribune*'s photo staff outnumbers St. Paul's bare-bones photo staff of two full-time and one half-time photojournalists by a wide margin (Orrick interview, April 26, 2018). Although the *Star Tribune* does not publish a great deal of video content because this is so time-intensive, Webster

The *Star Tribune*'s emphasis on visual journalism has presented many opportunities for photojournalist Brian Peterson to work on long-term projects. (Photo by Mary Lou Nemanic, 2015.)

noted their video content is both well-chosen and well-produced (Webster interview).

As far as still photography, the robust staff regularly create galleries and slideshows for the website that are quite popular with readers. Brian Peterson is a photojournalist hired by the newspaper in 1987. He has won numerous national and local awards, including the Robert F. Kennedy Photojournalism Award and awards from the National Press Photographers as well as being named nine times as Minnesota Press Photographer of the Year. He has had many opportunities over the years to work on long-term projects, including a documentary project that lasted from 1989 to 1996 about a southern Minnesota family afflicted with AIDS (Peterson interview). In 2015 the *Star Tribune* published *Minnesota State of Wonder*, a book with photographs by Peterson and text by travel editor Kerri Westenberg, based on a series that began in the Travel section of the newspaper.

While long-term planning is critical to maintaining a metro daily, given the evolving newsroom technology and practices, the

Star Tribune limits its long-term plans to two years (Edmonds 2016b). A major goal has been diversifying additional non-news revenue streams, which provided 10 percent of its revenue in 2016, and includes local printing work, particularly *USA Today* and the *Pioneer Press* (Edmonds 2016b). The newspaper also profits from its weekly arts, food, and entertainment tabloid, *City Pages,* which it purchased in 2015 and which brings in additional revenue by cosponsoring concerts, festivals, and other events with local businesses. A particular fiscal goal for the paper has been to achieve 50 percent of its revenue from advertising and 50 percent from readers. In 2012 the revenue from readers was up to 45 percent, and by 2018 up to 48 percent (Lisheron 2012; Klingensmith e-mail).

Calling this strategy a "revolutionary idea," a 2012 article in the *American Journalism Review* quoted analyst Robert Levine: "Very few newspapers have ever tried to sell news. The Minneapolis *Star Tribune* is in a very good competitive position because no one in its market delivers its news product like the Strib [*Star Tribune*] does" (Lisheron 2012).

Conclusion

With the long-term goal of strengthening its statewide coverage, which is weak in the northern and southern parts of the state, the *Star Tribune* continues to thrive under the benevolent ownership of Glen Taylor, while the *Pioneer Press* remains in survival mode in the hope of finding a locally based owner (Webster interview; Kelly interview). And while the rivalry between the *Pioneer Press* and the *Star Tribune* has diminished considerably, a comparison of the two newspapers reveals the importance of investment in print and online operations as part of an integrated multiplatform strategy that features visual journalism. It also illustrates the significance of experimentation in methods of storytelling as well as methods of revenue generation from non-news sources. The *Star Tribune* is indeed an excellent example of a thriving metro with a reputation for quality journalism. In contrast, it is disheartening to see my hometown paper, the scrappy, once-mighty *Pioneer Press,* stripped to the bone in pursuit of profit. Yet there is something readers of Alden's newspapers can do, according to Reynolds:

> I would tell people to definitely pay for that subscription because journalists need to be paid. But—*but*—I think the public needs to raise some hell. I think they need to let publishers, not editors, know that they're upset with the state of their newspaper. They need to be very vocal about that, and let local officials and politicians know that this is a civic issue in their community. So, yes, pay the money, but raise some hell with the people who can get word up to Alden. (Quoted in Hutchins 2018)

Conclusion

In Search of a Multiplatform Business Model

In the first two decades of the twenty-first century, the search for a sustainable business model for multiplatform news delivery has dominated scholarly and professional literature about the industry (Edge 2014a; Edmonds 2016b). In particular, the *New York Times* and the *Minneapolis Star Tribune* have been singled out for their best practices nationally and regionally and for their innovative business strategies.

In 2013 Ken Doctor, media analyst for Harvard's Nieman Lab, wrote an analysis of these two metro dailies. They both had the distinction of winning multiple Pulitzer Prizes that year: The *Times*, with a newsroom of 1,150, won four, and the *Star Tribune* just four years out of bankruptcy and with a newsroom of about 250—won two (Doctor 2013b). Significantly, despite newsroom cuts during the recession and its aftermath, these newspapers have maintained sizeable reporting staffs. In the case of the *Star Tribune*, Doctor noted that it kept "its reporting staff as whole as possible" by disproportionately cutting "copy handling and middle management" (Doctor 2013b). At the *Times*, despite some buyouts and layoffs starting in 2008 that reduced the newsroom size from more than 1,300 to more than 1,100, the last round of buyouts in 2017 reduced the editor pool so that the newspaper could increase its pool of reporters (Walters 2017).

In addition to continuing to invest in their print platforms, both metros have increasingly invested in their digital platforms, both adding new hires in the areas of multimedia and visual journalism (Doctor 2013b; *Star Tribune* interviews, 2018). Particularly significant at the *Times* in 2017 was the hiring of about a dozen visual journalists who specialized in photography, videography, or graphics (Benton 2017).

Overall, Doctor argues that there is a link between investment in quality journalism, as recognized by the Pulitzers, and the increasing profitability of both of these newspapers. He explains that, in order to break new ground in an era of declining advertising revenue and circulation, the industry needs "to understand how editorial quality and quantity play into the very revival of the newspaper *business*" and that quality content must be seen "as a *business* imperative" (2013b). Philip Meyer made this argument in 2009 for newspapers generally, presenting evidence that correlated journalistic credibility with profitability.

Doctor also notes that these newspapers operate under "two of the most successful all-access digital circulation strategies in the country" (2013b). Both have seen annual increases in their digital revenue and both have metered paywalls that allow readers to access their websites a few times before buying subscriptions. Additionally, both publications have periodically redesigned their websites to make them more user friendly and have created apps for mobile devices. In fact, in 2017, Doctor called the *New York Times'* set of smart-phone applications the first "newspaper-created product that seems utterly comfortable with the digital medium" (2016b). Redesigning digital applications for ease in readability is a key component within the *Times'* subscriber-first strategies that emphasize reader engagement. According to Doctor, with mobile applications, "The *Times* has found that about one out of eight digital readers drive[s] its business. . . . So engagement—more minutes, now especially in mobile[—]drives subscription sales, retention and the ability to increase prices over time" (2016b). In fact, CNBC reported that the *Times* was "the first news organization in the world to pass the 1 million digital-only subscription mark" (Ell 2018; Ember 2018).

In addition, *Times* digital subscriptions continued to increase, even after the "Trump Bump" of 2016 and early 2017 had ended (Doctor 2017b). The Trump Bump refers to the subscription boom that resulted from President Donald Trump's domination of the news that has also affected other news operations such as the *Washington Post,* ProPublica, and cable channels such as MSNBC and CNN (Doctor 2017b). This bump attracted more than half a million digital subscribers to the *Times,* many of whom it has been able to retain (*The Economist* 2017).

In contrast to the *New York Times,* while the publisher of the *Minneapolis Star Tribune* saw growth in digital subscriptions, he did not attribute that to the Trump Bump:

> The *Star Tribune* has continued to have strong growth in digital subscriptions in 2016 and 2017 (roughly 20% per year) but we do not attribute that to Trump's presidency. In fact, in our market, I view his presidency as depressive to digital volume rather than supportive, but that is not a provable assertion. (Klingensmith e-mail)

Significantly, both the *New York Times* and the *Star Tribune* have adopted evolving business models with the goal of decreasing reliance on advertising and focusing more on reader revenue (Doctor 2013b). In 2017 the *New York Times,* with its subscriber-first strategy, reported taking in 62 percent of its revenue from readers (Doctor 2017a; Spears 2018). Mike Klingensmith, publisher and CEO of the *Star Tribune,* wrote, "In the first half of 2018, 7% of our revenue comes from printing and distribution of third party publications. Of the remaining 93% of revenue, 48% of that comes from the reader and 52% comes from advertisers" (Klingensmith e-mail). In addition, both publications have increased their revenue streams with brand-sponsored events and through their online stores, which sell souvenir clothing, books, and gifts. In 2018 the *Star Tribune* reported that 10 percent of its reader income came from nontraditional revenue streams (Edmonds 2018). Two innovative examples of this include a program that gives companies and nonprofits opportunities to cosponsor its events, and a program for teams, clubs, and nonprofits to raise funds by selling subscriptions to the *Star Tribune.*

The *Star Tribune* has also generated revenue by offering short-term opportunities such as a photo workshop taught by a staff photojournalist during a local practice session of the U.S. Figure Skating Championships (Hare 2016). According to the newspaper's events manager, Steve Yaeger, while this did not bring in a great deal of revenue, "our costs were very low, engagement was off the charts and everyone involved asked us to do it again" (Hare 2016).

In the case of the *New York Times,* its array of non-news-branded events and programs is incredibly diverse, experimental, and profitable. In addition to the sale of framed prints of iconic photographs and branded gifts at its online store, a few of the many innovative events and programs promoted between 2016 and 2018 in *Times* print advertisements included the following:

- "New York Times Ultimate Birthday Book" of front pages from every year of a person's life
- One-day "Pre-College Symposium on College Admission" for students and parents
- "Meditation Journeys": a series of guided meditations set in four California locations presented in virtual reality
- "Times Journeys": more than 45 itineraries on 6 continents with *New York Times* experts, including "Flying in Zero Gravity at NASA"
- "New York Times Meal Cooking Kits"

Although both publications have numerous similarities, especially quality content, integrated multiplatform approaches, and an emphasis on visual journalism, a major distinction is in ownership. The *New York Times* is a media company with international assets, while, as detailed in Chapter 5, the *Star Tribune* is owned by billionaire Glen Taylor, the owner of the Minnesota Timberwolves professional basketball team. As a civic benefactor, Taylor has received acclaim for his hands-off management style and for arranging to convert the newspaper to nonprofit status after his death (Doctor 2013b). Other civic benefactors owning metro dailies include the *Washington Post*'s owner, Jeff Bezos, also owner of Amazon, and the *Boston Globe*'s owner, John Henry, also owner of the Boston Red Sox professional baseball team.

Like Taylor, Bezos, who bought the *Post* in 2013, has been detached from daily newsroom operations, but he has also encouraged experimentation, especially in video advertising (Lichterman 2017). Additionally, Bezos has increased the newsroom size substantially, to more than 800, adding approximately 60 new digital and video positions in 2017 and 2018 (Lichterman 2017; Fuller 2018). In recent years the newspaper has been so successful that between 2016 and 2018 digital subscriptions tripled to more than 1 million, and in 2017 the addition of 157,000 digital-only subscribers in the last quarter of that year pushed "overall subscription revenue to more than $1 billion for the year" (Fuller 2018; Ember 2018).

Nonprofit Ownership

While ownership of newspapers by civic benefactors has been possible for only a few metro dailies, another avenue of consideration for a sustainable business model has been the conversion to nonprofit status. Because nonprofit status does not require newspapers to make a profit, it appears to liberate a news outlet from expectations of increasing profitability; however, as evident at long term news operations such as the *MinnPost*, sustaining a nonprofit organization requires diversity in funding sources that typically include a mix of advertising, grants, and fundraising events and promotions. In addition, according to the *Columbia Journalism Review*, fundraising strategies should include national as well as local sources because "relying solely on local money increases the risk that the nonprofits will offend donors when stories hit too close to home" (Lee 2017).

Complicating nonprofit status for news outlets is the fact that foundations frequently offer grants for specific investigative and long-term projects, making journalists vulnerable to a foundation's specific imperatives and interests. Nicholas Lemann, former dean of Columbia University's Journalism School, told the Poynter Institute's Rick Edmonds that while nonprofit news sites such as ProPublica and the *Texas Tribune* have been compensating for the lack of investigative reporting by traditional media, they face ethical concerns different from those of news operations supported by advertising:

> Traditional major newspaper advertisers, like department stores and auto dealers, didn't want to have a conversation about what work the City Hall reporter would be doing before they signed a contract, because the reporter usually wasn't going to be covering their business. But that's exactly the kind of conversation donors to news nonprofits want to have about the reporter on campaign finance, or education reform, or environmental policy, before they decide whether the gift they're being asked for fits their mission. (Quoted in Edmonds 2016a)

Consequently, the American Press Institute has issued a call for a code of ethics governing the funding of specific stories (Edmonds 2016a). In addition, Edmonds notes that National Public Radio's (NPR's) news policy provides a good model to consider. His description is based on NPR's news policy manual:

> Here's a journalistic proposition: it would be ethical for a reporter to accept a grant from the Ford Foundation for coverage of Eastern Europe. After all, Ford has a distinguished record of funding projects that promote the study of foreign affairs but does not lobby or advocate specific policies. But it would be wrong to accept a grant

> from General Motors to cover international trade. Even were there no editorial interference, GM's economic interests in the matter would create a perceived conflict of interest. (Edmonds 2016a)

One of the oldest newspapers under the nonprofit umbrella is the *Tampa Bay Times.* Originally known as the *St. Petersburg Times,* it was renamed in 2012. The *St. Petersburg Times* was a biweekly newspaper bought by publisher Paul Poynter in 1912 and eventually published as a daily. Upon the death of Poynter's son, Nelson, in 1978, the *Tampa Bay Times* was willed to the nonprofit Poynter Institute for Media Studies (Danielson 2016). The newspaper is known for its investigative work and has won twelve Pulitzer Prizes since 1964, including two in 2009. The *Tampa Bay Times* also created politifact.com, a website for journalists to fact-check statements by government officials and special interest groups. In 2016 the *Tampa Bay Times* bought out its competitor, the *Tampa Bay Tribune,* and then closed the newspaper. According to *Times* CEO Paul Tash, the city could not sustain two daily newspapers (Danielson 2016). However, prior to its closure, the condition of the *Tampa Bay Tribune* under its hedge fund owner, Revolution Capital, provided a good illustration of the threat hedge funds pose to the newspaper industry. In 2012, when Revolution purchased it, the *Tampa Tribune*'s newsroom was at 618 employees, but by 2016 the staff was down to less than half, at 265. Also that year, after selling the *Tampa Bay Tribune*'s building for $17.75 million, Revolution sold the newspaper to the *Tampa Bay Times* (Benton 2016).

Probably one of the most unique nonprofit arrangements involves three of Philadelphia's for-profit news outlets—the *Philadelphia Inquirer,* the *Philadelphia Daily News,* and the website philly.com—all of which are owned by a nonprofit trust. In 2016, after several years of declining advertising profits, decreasing circulation revenue, seven different owners in eleven years, bankruptcy, and several rounds of layoffs, the news outlets' owner, philanthropist Gerry Lenfest, gifted them to the nonprofit Lenfest Institute (Hare 2017b). The institute is a "first-of-its-kind non-profit organization whose sole mission is to develop and support sustainable business models for great local journalism" (Lenfest Institute n.d.). According to the institute's website, the three news outlets operate for profit as a "public-benefit corporation" under the institute's nonprofit umbrella, which, according to media analyst Rem Rieder, "means no public shareholders and no scrutiny from security analysts" (Lenfest Institute n.d.; Rieder 2017). Further,

> these news properties now serve as a live lab for the Institute's innovation efforts. The Institute is overseen by a Board of Managers . . . [and] are now the largest newspapers in America operated as a public-benefit corporation, under the non-profit ownership of the Institute, dedicated solely to the mission of preserving local journalism nationwide. These news properties will also serve as a live lab for the Institute's innovation investments. With this organizational structure in place, the endowment for the Institute is able to receive additional donations from individuals, foundations, corporations and other entities for the mission of continuing journalism, all of which are tax-deductible through The Philadelphia Foundation. (Lenfest Institute n.d.)

Originally established with an endowment of $20 million from Lenfest, the institute announced that in 2017 it had raised an additional $26.5 million from a variety of sources and that this had convinced Lenfest to contribute another $40 million to the institute (Rieder 2017; Knight Foundation 2017). Also, in 2017, the institute unveiled a national program for news innovation with $1 million in grants to support "new approaches to sustaining local journalism in Philadelphia and similar metro regions around the U.S." (Lenfest Institute 2017).

The Lenfest Institute, a major supporter of local news, is involved in collaborations with several other nonprofit organizations, especially the Knight Foundation. These collaborations include the Knight-Lenfest Newsroom Initiative (formerly

Knight-Temple Table Stakes Project), which is dedicated to developing digital best practices, increasing digital subscriptions, and improving their community engagement (Knight Foundation 2017). The Knight-Lenfest collaboration also supports the Knight-Lenfest News Transformation Fund to help transform and strengthen local journalism in the digital age, and Report for America, which was established in 2017 by a partnership between the GroundTruth Project and Google News Lab (Brown 2019; GroundTruth Project 2019). Report for America provides understaffed newsrooms across the country with journalists in yearlong residencies and is also funded by other nonprofits supporting local news, such as the Facebook Journalism Project (Brown 2019; GroundTruth Project 2019).

In terms of longevity, an outstanding example of a nonprofit news outlet is the *MinnPost,* a digital newspaper founded in 2007 "for people who care about Minnesota" (Konieczna 2014). Although *MinnPost* is not a metro daily, it is often identified as an outstanding model of a sustainable news outlet (Knight Foundation 2011; Konieczna 2014). It was founded by former *Minneapolis Star Tribune* editor and publisher, Joel Kramer, and his partner, Laurie Kramer, to fill in the gaps in local reporting in the Twin Cities area at a time when the *Star Tribune* and the *Pioneer Press* had laid off approximately one hundred staff members (Konieczna 2014). This allowed the Kramers to staff *MinnPost* with journalists who had been bought out or had retired.

According to a Knight Foundation report on nonprofit news operations, *MinnPost* "achieved the greatest revenue diversity among the sites studied" (Knight Foundation 2011). On the basis of the strategies for public radio funding, Kramer reported that *MinnPost*'s revenue breakdown in 2011 included advertising at 25 percent, donations at 37 percent, foundation grants at 37 percent, and consulting at 1 percent (reported in Konieczna 2014, 54). Despite the diversity of funding sources, *MinnPost*'s goal was to reduce its dependence on foundation funding to 10 percent (Konieczna 2014, 54). To this end, Kramer stated that 80–85 percent of *MinnPost*'s revenue in 2016 came from a mix of "business-related revenue streams, which are mainly memberships and major donors and advertising and sponsorships" (quoted in Wang 2016). Included in *MinnPost*'s donations category is an annual event, a dinner and variety show called MinnRoast, that in 2014 drew 1,400 people and brought in $160,000—10 percent of *MinnPost*'s annual budget (Batsell 2014; Konieczna 2014).

Significantly, because of concern for journalistic autonomy, *MinnPost*'s practice is to first identify the subject to cover and then seek grants to fund its coverage, rather than first identifying what funders are interested in and then determining the subject on the basis of their funding criteria (Knight Foundation 2011). In 2013 *MinnPost*, the *Texas Tribune*, and the *Voice of San Diego* were singled out by the Knight Foundation as particularly successful at decreasing their reliance on grants through advertising, syndication, and developing corporate sponsorships (Knight Foundation 2013).

Ensuring the Survival of Metro Dailies

While a standard business model for the sustainability of metro dailies has yet to be developed, successful business strategies emphasize reliance on a diversity of revenue sources and decreasing dependence on advertising. In addition, quality content is critical for engaging and retaining subscribers across platforms as are major commitments to public service and to visual journalism. Through branded non-news events, programs, and gifts, metro dailies can also develop increasingly significant revenue streams to compensate for declining advertising revenue.

Overall, the evidence leads me to reject both Digital-First and printcentric approaches to content delivery and to advocate for what the *St. Paul Pioneer Press*'s staff calls "Digital Right." As noted earlier, this involves debuting content on the platform most appropriate to the complexity of the story and having the ability to reach the largest number of readers via the platform on a particular day (e.g., Sunday versus a weekday) or at a particular time of day. In addition, to meet the challenge of integrating the practices of print and digital journalism, I recommend adopting a hybrid approach to content delivery similar to that of the *Minneapolis Star Tribune.* Central to its newsroom organization is a Quick Strike Team, a unit dedicated to fast-breaking news that updates the website frequently with brief stories. This structure gives multimedia teams and beat reporters time to concentrate on detailed and more analytical content across platforms that preserves print journalism's values of verification, balance, and in-depth coverage.

Significantly, as detailed in this book's case studies, newspapers have the best chance for success when owners allow journalists to manage their newspapers to ensure production of quality journalism under the protection of newspaper guilds. This is evident at the *Minneapolis Star Tribune,* where the owner, a civic benefactor, refrains from interfering in its daily operations.

Particularly problematic is the current trend of hedge fund and corporate owners that are preoccupied with quarterly profits and realize profitability through layoffs and resource cutbacks that are jeopardizing quality standards. In addition, journalistic autonomy is eroding under the establishment of quotas and pressure from ideological and commercial influences. This autonomy has been safeguarded by newspaper guild representation, which is also under siege as some corporate owners use the industry's crisis as an opportunity to disable or eliminate it.

Overall, while my research has not enabled me to predict the lifespan for print, it is clear that so far newspapers have defied decades of doomsday predictions. Despite annual declines in print advertising, it still provides the largest share of advertising profits for many metros across the country. In 2018 CEO Mark Thompson said this of the *New York Times*: "I believe at least 10 years is what we can see in the U.S. for our print products" (quoted in Ell 2018). Others are even more optimistic, predicting newspapers can survive for niche audiences and for publication of commemorative editions rather than completely give way to the digital side (Sambrook 2017).

Despite some of the optimistic possibilities for sustaining newspapers, if they are to survive, many newspapers will need to rebuild after having been decimated by cuts in staff and resources. As the Pew Research Center reported, between 2007 and 2017, 45 percent—almost half—of U.S. newspaper staffs were scaled back (Grieco 2018). This incredible statistic has alarmed analysts and scholars alike. In response to Pew's revelation, *Washington Post* media columnist Margaret Sullivan wrote:

> The dire numbers play out in ugly ways: Public officials aren't held accountable, town budgets go unscrutinized, experienced journalists are working at Walmart, or not at all, instead of plying their trade in their communities. One problem with losing local coverage is that we never know what we don't know. Corruption can flourish, taxes can rise, public officials can indulge their worst impulses. And there's another result that gets less attention: In our terribly divided nation, we need the local newspaper to give us common information—an agreed-upon set of facts to argue about. (Sullivan 2018a, C1)

As Julie Reynolds has emphasized in her reports on hedge fund ownership, it is not enough that readers become aware of what hedge funds are doing to their local newspapers; instead of canceling their subscriptions, "the public needs to raise some hell," because preserving local newspapers is essential to our democracy (quoted in Hutchins 2018).

Interviews and Correspondence

Bjorhus, Jen, watchdog reporter, *Minneapolis Star Tribune*. Tape-recorded telephone interview by the author, May 4, 2018.

Buffalo News reporters and photojournalists who requested anonymity. Interviews by the author, 2015–2018.

Chan, Gus, photojournalist, *Cleveland Plain Dealer*. Tape-recorded telephone interview by the author, March 14, 2014.

Christmann, Samantha, business reporter, *Buffalo News*. Tape-recorded interview by the author, Buffalo, New York, December 15, 2015; tape-recorded telephone interviews by the author, May 17, 2016, and February 25, 2018; and e-mail correspondence, November 25, 2018.

Connolly, Brian, vice president of innovation and business development, *Buffalo News*. Tape-recorded interview by the author, Buffalo, New York, December 15, 2015, and tape-recorded telephone interview by the author, August 2, 2017.

Curtiss, Cathaleen, director of photography, *Buffalo News*. Tape-recorded telephone interview by the author, August 8, 2017.

Denney, Dave, assigning editor and photo editor, *Minneapolis Star Tribune*. Tape-recorded telephone interview by the author, June 8, 2018.

DeYoung, Lisa, photojournalist, *Cleveland Plain Dealer*. Tape-recorded telephone interview by the author, October 15, 2014.

Dissell, Rachel, investigative reporter, *Plain Dealer*. Tape-recorded interview by the author, Cleveland, Ohio, September 28, 2015.

Dolan, Mark, *National Press Photographers*. Tape-recorded telephone interviews by the author, November 1, 2014, and February 15, 2016.

Fladung, Thom, former managing editor, *Cleveland Plain Dealer*. Tape-recorded interview by the author, Cleveland, Ohio, September 28, 2015.

Gehrz, Jim, photojournalist, *Minneapolis Star Tribune*. Tape-recorded telephone interviews by the author, March 25, 2013, and June 30, 2015, and follow-up e-mail correspondence, March 13, 2015.

Kelly, Colleen, senior digital editor, *Minneapolis Star Tribune*. Tape-recorded telephone interview by the author, June 19, 2018.

Klingensmith, Michael, publisher and CEO, *Minneapolis Star Tribune*. E-mail correspondence, September 5, 2018.

Kordalski, David, former assistant managing editor for visuals, *Cleveland Plain Dealer*. Tape-recorded interview by the author, Cleveland, Ohio, September 29, 2015, and tape-recorded telephone interview by the author, March 20, 2016.

Lakamp, Patrick, data-driven enterprise editor/reporter, *Buffalo News*. Tape-recorded interview by the author, Buffalo, New York, December 15, 2015.

Lambert, Neal, team leader and editor, Photography Department, *St. Paul Pioneer Press*. Tape-recorded interview by the author, St. Paul, Minnesota, May 18, 2015.

LaVigne, Michelle, former photojournalist, *Chicago Sun-Times*. Tape-recorded telephone interview by the author, February 25, 2015.

McManamon, Wendy, copyeditor, *Cleveland Plain Dealer*. Tape-recorded interview by the author, Cleveland, Ohio, September 29, 2015; tape-recorded telephone interviews by the author, February 7, 2016, and March 17, 2016; and e-mail correspondence, November 23, 2018.

Meehan, Sara, digital news editor, *Buffalo News*. Tape-recorded telephone interview by the author, May 22, 2016.

Orrick, Dave, state government and politics reporter (former outdoor writer/photographer), *St. Paul Pioneer Press*. Tape-recorded interview by the author, St. Paul, Minnesota, May 18, 2015, and tape-recorded telephone interview by the author, April 26, 2018.

O'Shei, Tim, feature writer, *Buffalo News*. Tape-recorded telephone interview by the author, February 16, 2017.

Pastner, Deb, director of photo/multimedia, *Minneapolis Star Tribune*. Tape-recorded interview by the author, Minneapolis, Minnesota, August 19, 2015.

Peterson, Brian, photojournalist, *Minneapolis Star Tribune*. Tape-recorded interview by the author, Minneapolis, Minnesota, August 19, 2015.

Pinkley, Jenni, senior video editor, *Minneapolis Star Tribune*. Tape-recorded telephone interview by the author, August 13, 2015.

Plain Dealer reporters and photojournalists who requested anonymity. Interviews by the author, 2015–2019.

Rendleman, Julia, former photojournalist, *Pittsburgh Post-Gazette*. Tape-recorded telephone interviews by the author, August 18, 2015, and June 7, 2018.

Rodrigue, George, president and editor, *Cleveland Plain Dealer*. Tape recorded interview by the author, Cleveland, Ohio, September 28, 2015.

Sanina, Mila, former deputy managing editor, *Pittsburgh Post-Gazette*. Tape recorded interview by the author, Pittsburgh, Pennsylvania, August 18, 2015; tape-recorded telephone interview by the author, March 5, 2018; and e-mail correspondence, June 8, 2018.

Shribman, David, executive editor, *Pittsburgh Post-Gazette*. Tape-recorded interview by the author, Pittsburgh, Pennsylvania, August 8, 2015, and tape-recorded telephone interview by the author, October 21, 2016.

Silver, Jon, investigative reporter and assignment editor, *Pittsburgh Post-Gazette*. Tape-recorded interview by the author, Pittsburgh, Pennsylvania, March 6, 2018, and tape-recorded telephone interview by the author, August 18, 2015.

Star Tribune reporters and photojournalists who requested anonymity. Interviews by the author, 2015–2018.

Strasburg, Stephanie, photojournalist/multimedia storyteller, *Pittsburgh Post-Gazette*. Tape-recorded telephone interview by the author, April 24, 2018.

Sullivan, Margaret, media columnist *Washington Post* (former editor and vice president, *Buffalo News*). Tape-recorded telephone interview by the author, June 15, 2016.

Tan, Sandy, reporter and Newsguild president, *Buffalo News*. Tape-recorded telephone interview by the author, June 7, 2018.

Tsujimoto, Ben, digital content coordinator, *Buffalo News*. Tape-recorded telephone interviews by the author, June 9, 2016, and March 5, 2018.

Webster, MaryJo, computer-assisted reporting editor, *Minneapolis Star Tribune*. Tape-recorded telephone interview by the author, May 11, 2018.

Westpfahl, Jen, former deputy editor, digital news and social media, *St. Paul Pioneer Press*. Tape-recorded interview by the author, St. Paul, Minnesota, May 18, 2015, and tape-recorded telephone interview by the author, April 3, 2018.

Winslow, Donald, former executive editor of *News Photographer* magazine for the National Press Photographers Association. E-mail correspondence, July 22, 2016.

References

Adams, Russell, Shira Ovide, and Stephanie Simon. 2009. "*Rocky Mountain News* folds amid ad slump." *Wall Street Journal*, February 27, 2009. Accessed July 24, 2016. http://www.wsj.com/articles/SB123567732712586001.

AFL-CIO New York City Central Labor Council. 2014. "TNG, allies rally against *El Diario* layoffs." August 22, 2014. Accessed June 8, 2017. http://www.nycclc.org/news/2014-08/tng-allies-rally-against-el-diario-layoffs.

Allan, Stuart. 2013. *Citizen witnessing: Revisioning journalism in times of crisis*. Cambridge, MA: Polity Press.

Allan, Stuart, and Einar Thorsen, eds. 2009. *Citizen journalism: Global perspectives*. Vol. 1. New York: Peter Lang.

Alliance for Audited Media. 2016. "Circulation figures for the *Plain Dealer*." March 2016. Accessed March 31, 2016. https://auditedmedia.com.

Andén-Papadopoulos, Kari, and Mervi Pantti, eds. 2011. *Amateur images and global news*. Bristol, UK: Intellect Books.

———. 2013. "Re-imagining crisis reporting: Professional ideology of journalists and citizen eyewitness images." *Journalism* 14 (7): 960–977.

Anderson, C. W. 2011. "Between creative and quantified audiences: Web metrics and changing patterns of newswork in local US newsrooms." *Journalism* 12 (5): 550–566.

———. 2013. *Rebuilding the news: Metropolitan journalism in the digital age*. Philadelphia: Temple University Press.

Anderson, Monica. 2013. "At newspapers, photographers feel the brunt of job cuts." Pew Research Center, November 11, 2013. Accessed July 15, 2016. http://www.pewresearch.org/fact-tank/2013/11/11/at-newspapers-photographers-feel-the-brunt-of-job-cuts/.

Associated Press. 2010. "Pew Research Center study finds newspapers provide the majority of original news reporting." January 11, 2010. Accessed May 3, 2017. http://www.masslive.com/news/index.ssf/2010/01/pew_research_center_study_find.html.

———. 2013. "*Chicago Sun-Times* lays off all of its full-time photographers." *New York Times*, May 31, 2013. Accessed July 15, 2016. http://www.nytimes.com/2013/06/01/business/media/chicago-sun-times-lays-off-all-its-full-time-photographers.html?_r=0.

Atkins, Annette. 2018. "St. Paul, Minneapolis, and Minnesota's urban origins." MNopedia, February 28, 2018. Accessed July 9, 2018. http://www.mnopedia.org/st-paul-minneapolis-and-minnesotas-urban-origins.

Avilés, José Alberto García, and Miguel Carvajal. 2008. "Integrated and cross-media newsroom convergence: Two models of multimedia news production—the cases of Novotecnica and La Verdad Multimedia in Spain." *Convergence* 14 (2): 221–239.

Bailey, Holly. 2013. "At Visa Pour l'Image, proof that photojournalism isn't dead." yahoo.com, September 2, 2013. Accessed July 15, 2016. http://news.yahoo.com/at-visa-pour-l-image—proof-that-photojournalism-isn-t-dead-205451904.html.

Barthel, Michael. 2015a. "Newspaper circulation falls in 2014." Pew Research Center for Journalism and Media, April 28, 2015. Accessed March 25, 2016. http://www.journalism.org/chart/newspaper-circulation-falls-in-2014/.

———. 2015b. "Newspapers: Fact sheet." Pew Research Center for Journalism and Media, April 29, 2015. Accessed March 25, 2016. http://www.journalism.org/2015/04/29/newspapers-fact-sheet/.

———. 2016. "Newspapers: Fact sheet." Pew Research Center for Journalism and Media, June 15, 2016. Accessed June 16, 2016. http://www.journalism.org/2016/06/15/newspapers-fact-sheet/.

Batsell, Jake. 2014. "Monetizing the fun factor: How upbeat events can build engagement and boost the bottom line." NewsBiz, April 2014. Accessed August 24, 2018. http://news-biz.org/post/84435323853/monetizing-the-fun-factor-how-upbeat-events-can.

Beaujon, Andrew. 2013. "Mich. unions say JRC has 'declared war,' threaten strike." Poynter Institute, March 1, 2013. Accessed June 8, 2017. http://www.poynter.org/2013/mich-unions-say-jrc-has-declared-war-threaten-strike/205855/.

Beaujon, Andrew, Kristen Hare, Sam Kirkland, and Benjamin Mullin. 2014. "How mass layoffs in 2013 changed the lives of former *Plain Dealer* staffers." Poynter Institute, July 31, 2014. Accessed November 30, 2015. http://www.poynter.org/news/mediawire/260863/how-mass-layoffs-in-2013-changed-the-lives-of-former-plain-dealer-staffers/.

Bechmann, Anja. 2011. "Closer apart? The networks of cross-media news production." In *Making online news*. Vol. 2, edited by David Domingo and Chris A. Paterson, 15–28. New York: Peter Lang.

Becker, Karin. 2004. "Where is visual culture in contemporary theories of media and communication?" *Nordicom Review* 25 (1–2): 149–157.

Belz, Adam. 2014. "Glen Taylor finalizes purchase of Star Tribune." Star Tribune, July 1, 2014. Accessed July 27, 2018. http://www.startribune.com/july-1-2014-glen-taylor-finalizes-purchase-of-star-tribune/265223641/.

Benton, Joshua. 2016. "Tampa just lost a daily newspaper; is this the continuation of an old trend or the start of a new one?" Nieman Lab, May 4, 2016. Accessed August 16, 2018. http://www.niemanlab.org/2016/05/tampa-just-lost-a-daily-newspaper-is-this-the-continuation-of-an-old-trend-or-the-start-of-a-new-one.

———. 2017. "This is The New York Times' digital path forward." Nieman Lab, January 17, 2017. Accessed December 19, 2017. http://www.niemanlab.org/2017/01/this-is-the-new-york-times-digital-path-forward/.

Bever, Lindsey. 2013. "Journalism's future in focus as *Chicago Sun-Times* shutters photographers." *The Guardian,* June 5, 2013. Accessed July 15, 2016. http://www.theguardian.com/commentisfree/2013/jun/05/journalism-chicago-suntimes-photographers/print.

Block, John Robinson. 2008. "*Post-Gazette* opinion pages: Meet the Editorial Board." *Pittsburgh Post-Gazette,* June 19, 2008. Accessed May 23, 2018. http://www.post-gazette.com/opinion/2008/06/19/Post-Gazette-Opinion-pages/stories/200806190235.

Boczkowski, Pablo J. 2004. *Digitizing the news: Innovation in online newspapers.* Cambridge, MA: MIT Press.

———. 2010. *News at work: Imitation in an age of information abundance.* Chicago: University of Chicago Press.

Brady, Jim. 2016. "Local news isn't dead. We just need to stop killing it." *Columbia Journalism Review,* June 17, 2016. Accessed June 17, 2016. http://www.cjr.org/analysis/local_news_newspaper_print_business_model.php.

Bressers, Bonnie. 2006. "Promise and reality: The integration of print and online versions of major metropolitan newspapers." *International Journal on Media Management* 8 (3): 134–145.

Britton, Barney. 2012. 'No future in photojournalism' interview: Dan Chung." *Digital Photography Preview,* February 10, 2012. Accessed November 1, 2014. http://www.dpreview.com/articles/9982656990/no-future-in-photojournalism-interview-dan-chung.

Brown, Campbell. 2019. "Doing more to support local news." Facebook Journalism Project, January 15. Accessed July 26, 2019. https://facebookjournalismproject.com/article/doing-more-to-support-local-news/.

Brown-Smith, Carrie, and Jonathan Groves. 2016. "The lean newsroom: A roadmap for change." October 25, 2016. Accessed May 5, 2017. leannewsroom.com.

Brüggemann, Michael, Edda Humprecht, Rasmus Kleis Nielsen, Kari Karppinen, Alessio Cornia, and Frank Esser. 2016. "Framing the newspaper crisis: How debates on the state of the press are shaped in Finland, France, Germany, Italy, United Kingdom and United States." *Journalism Studies* 17 (5): 533–551.

Bruns, Axel. 2005. *Gatewatching: Collaborative online news production.* New York: Peter Lang.

Bucher, Hans-Jürgen, and Peter Schumacher. 2006. "The relevance of attention for selecting news content. An eye-tracking study on attention patterns in the reception of print and online media." *Communications* 31 (3): 347–368.

Bucholtz, Andrew 2016. "Cleveland Plain Dealer blasted for fake NBA story, lack of road MLB reporters." Awful Announcing, April 13, 2016. Accessed July 28, 2016. http://awfulannouncing.com/2016/cleveland-plain-dealer-blasted-for-fake-nba-story-lack-of-road-mlb-reporters.html.

Buehner, Tara. 2011. "Exposing the news hound: A study on the normative structure and routines of citizen photojournalists." Paper presented at the Association for the Education in Journalism and Mass Communication conference, August, St. Louis, Missouri.

Buffalo News. 2018. "#EveryDayAPhoto: Celebrating the beauty of Western New York." May 29, 2018. Accessed May 29, 2018. http://buffalonews.com/a-photo-a-day/.

Buffalo Newspaper Guild. 2018. "Company updates employees on State of the News." June 8, 2018. Accessed June 13, 2018. http://www.buffaloguild.org/2018/06/08/buyouts-result-in-painful-newsroom-losses.

Burgess, Neil. 2010. "For God's sake, somebody call it!" Editorial Photographers UK, August 1, 2010. Accessed November 1, 2014. http://www.epuk.org/opinion/for-gods-sake-somebody-call-it.

Burris, Keith. 2018. "One writer's roots: We're merging the editorial boards of the *Pittsburgh Post-Gazette* and *The (Toledo) Blade*." *Pittsburgh Post-Gazette,* March 4, 2018. Accessed March 27, 2018. http://www.post-gazette.com/opinion/Op-Ed/2018/03/04/We-re-merging-the-editorial-boards-of-the-Pittsburgh-Post-Gazette-and-The-Toledo-Blade/stories/201803040082.

Burton, Tom. 2017. "Photo staff helps *Buffalo News* produce live special section of police officer's funeral." National Press Photographers, November 3, 2017. Accessed January 26, 2018. https://nppa.org/news/buffalo-news-officer-funeral-special-section.

Buttry, Steve. 2016. "The newspaper industry's colossal mistake was a defensive digital strategy." *The Buttry Diary* (blog), October 18, 2016. Accessed May 9, 2017. https://stevebuttry.wordpress.com/2016/10/18/the-newspaper-industrys-colossal-mistake-was-a-defensive-digital-strategy/.

Calderone, Michael. 2018. "Editorial backing Trump in 'shithole' controversy sparks outrage: Pittsburgh Post-Gazette owner ordered the paper to run an editorial defending president on racism charge." *Politico,* January 18, 2018. Accessed March 25, 2018. https://www.politico.com/story/2018/01/18/trump-pittsburgh-post-gazette-editorial-shithole-346845.

Campbell, David. 2010. "Dead or alive? The state of photojournalism." David Campbell, October 5, 2010. Accessed July 15, 2016. https://www.david-campbell.org/2010/10/05/dead-or-alive-the-state-of-photojournalism/.

Cardin, Benjamin. 2009. "With no newspapers, as Thomas Jefferson knew, democracy suffers." *US News and World Report,* May 4, 2009. Accessed

July 24, 2016. http://www.usnews.com/opinion/articles/2009/05/04/with-no-newspapers-as-thomas-jefferson-knew-democracy-suffers.

Cartier-Bresson, Henri. 1952. *The decisive moment*. New York: Simon and Schuster.

Carvajal, Miguel, and José A. García Avilés. 2008. "From newspapers to multimedia groups: Business growth strategies of the regional press in Spain." *Journalism Practice* 2 (3): 453–462.

Case Western Reserve University. 1997. "*Plain Dealer*." In *Encyclopedia of Cleveland history*. Accessed November 24, 2015. http://ech.case.edu/cgi/article.pl?id=GJW.

Cavna, Michael. 2018. "Pittsburgh Post-Gazette's spiked anti-Trump cartoons will get a D.C. museum exhibit." *Washington Post*, June 29, 2018. Accessed June 30, 2018. https://www.washingtonpost.com/news/comic-riffs/wp/2018/06/29/pittsburgh-post-gazettes-spiked-anti-trump-car toons-will-get-a-d-c-museum-exhibit/?utm_term=.f12ecba4ac8f.

Chittum, Ryan. 2013a. "The Advance Publications name game." *Columbia Journalism Review*, June 19, 2013. Accessed December 28, 2015. https://archives.cjr.org/the_audit/the_oregonian_readies_the_guil.php?page=2.

———. 2013b. "The *Advocate* vs. the *Times-Picayune*." *Columbia Journalism Review*, April 30, 2013. Accessed May 14, 2017. http://archives.cjr.org/the_audit/the_advocate_vs_the_times-pica.php.

Christiansen, Clayton. 1997. *The innovator's dilemma*. Boston: Harvard Business School Press.

Chyi, Hsiang Iris. 2013. *Trial and error: US newspapers' digital struggles toward inferiority*. Pomplona, Spain: Department of Media Management, University of Navarra.

Chyi, Hsiang Iris, and Ori Tenenboim. 2017. "Reality check: Multiplatform newspaper readership in the United States, 2007–2015." *Journalism Practice* 11 (7): 798–819.

Cillizza, Chris. 2018. "Trump's 'shithole' comment is his new rock bottom." CNN, January 12, 2018. Accessed March 29, 2018. https://www.cnn.com/2018/01/11/politics/trump-rock-bottom/index.html.

Clark, Anna. 2013. "I am alive at the *Plain Dealer*." *Columbia Journalism Review*, July 31, 2013. Accessed November 19, 2015. http://www.cjr.org/united_states_project/cuts_at_cleveland_plain_dealer claim_50_journalists.php?page=all.

———. 2014a. "Beat transfers prompt new labor questions at *The Plain Dealer*." *Columbia Journalism Review*, September 24, 2014. Accessed December 27, 2015. http://www.cjr.org/united_states_project/plain_dealer_courts_beats_move.php.

———. 2014b. "Grief and grievances at *The Plain Dealer*: Advance's paper in Cleveland is embroiled in a labor dispute as it charts a new digital path." *Columbia Journalism Review*, February 13, 2014. Accessed March 28, 2016. http://www.cjr.org/united_states_project/newspaper_guild_files_nlrb_charge_against_plain_dealer.php.

———. 2014c. "This used to be a newsroom—the scene at the *Cleveland Plain Dealer.*" *Columbia Journalism Review,* January 17, 2014. Accessed November 19, 2015. http://www.cjr.org/united_states_project/newsroom_culture_is_gone_at_cleveland_plain_dealer.php.

———. 2014d. "What a Cleveland news outlet should learn from its flawed Tamir Rice coverage. The Northeast Ohio Media Group faces criticism from readers, and from fellow journalists." *Columbia Journalism Review,* December 2, 2014. Accessed January 29, 2016. http://www.cjr.org/local_news/tamir_rice_northeast_ohio_media_group.php.

Coester, Dana. 2017. "A matter of space: Designing newsrooms for new digital practice." American Press Institute, October 18, 2017. Accessed December 6, 2017. https://www.americanpressinstitute.org/publications/reports/strategy-studies/spaces-identify-problem/.

Cohen, Kris R. 2005. "What does the photoblog want?" *Media, Culture and Society* 27 (6): 883–901.

Collins, Bob. 2016. "Why didn't anyone save the Pioneer Press?" *Newscut* (blog), May 12, 2016. Accessed July 22, 2018. https://blogs.mprnews.org/newscut/2016/05/why-didnt-anyone-save-the-pioneer-press/.

Connelly, Mike. 2018. "Mike Connelly: What happens when a newspaper runs out of paper?" *Buffalo News,* May 6, 2018. Accessed September 15, 2018. https://buffalonews.com/2018/05/06/mike-connelly-what-happens-when-a-newspaper-runs-out-of-paper/.

Danielson, Richard. 2016. "Tampa Bay Times borrowed $13.3 million to finance Tribune purchase." *Tampa Bay Times,* May 4, 2016. Accessed August 16, 2018. http://www.tampabay.com/news/business/corporate/tampa-bay-times-borrowed-133-million-to-finance-tribune-purchase/2275912.

Dealbook. 2009. "Rocky Mountain News is shutting down." *New York Times,* February 26, 2009. Accessed March 5, 2017. https://dealbook.nytimes.com/2009/02/26/rocky-mountain-news-to-shut-down/?_r=0.

Deitch, Charlie. 2018. "*Pittsburgh Post-Gazette* appointment of new editorial-page editor will make things worse." *Pittsburgh City Paper,* March 7, 2018. Accessed March 27, 2018. https://www.pghcitypaper.com/pittsburgh/pittsburgh-post-gazette-appointment-of-new-editorial-page-editor-will-make-things-worse/Content?oid=6992817.

Deppen, Colin. 2018a. "AARP received complaints about the *Pittsburgh Post-Gazette*'s 'bizarre' ad campaign." theincline.com, September 7, 2018. Accessed December 19, 2018. https://theincline.com/2018/09/07/aarp-received-complaints-about-the-pittsburgh-post-gazettes-bizarre-ad-campaign/.

———. 2018b. "The Pittsburgh Post-Gazette no longer prints a daily newspaper." theincline.com, August 26, 2018. Accessed December 19, 2018. https://theincline.com/2018/08/26/the-pittsburgh-post-gazette-no-longer-prints-a-daily-newspaper/.

Deuze, Mark. 2004. "What is multimedia journalism?" *Journalism Studies* 5 (2): 139–152.

Devega, Chauncey. 2018. "When a cartoonist becomes a hero: Rob Rogers on losing his job for making fun of Donald Trump." *Salon,* June 25, 2018. Accessed Junc 28, 2018. https://www.salon.com/2018/06/25/when-a-cartoonist-becomes-a-hero-rob-rogers-on-getting-fired-over-his-trump-caricatures/.

DFM Workers. 2018. "News Guild website representing 13 newspapers owned by Digital First Media." DFM Workers, 2018. Accessed July 15, 2018. https://dfmworkers.org/about/.

Diddlebock, Bob. 2009. "Who really killed the *Rocky Mountain News*?" *Time,* March 6, 2009. Accessed July 22, 2016. http://content.time.com/time/business/article/0,8599,1883345,00.html.

Doctor, Ken. 2012. "The Newsonomics of Advance's New Orleans strategy." Nieman Lab, October 4, 2012. Accessed May 14, 2017. http://www.niemanlab.org/2012/10/the-newsonomics-of-advances-new-orleans-strategy/.

———. 2013a. "The Newsonomics of Advance's advancing strategy and its Achilles' heel." Nieman Lab, June 27, 2013. Accessed May 14, 2017. http://www.niemanlab.org/2012/10/the-newsonomics-of-advances-new-orleans-strategy/.

———. 2013b. "The Newsonomics of Pulitzers, paywalls, and investing in the newsroom." Nieman Lab, April 18, 2013. Accessed July 26, 2018. http://www.niemanlab.org/2013/04/the-newsonomics-of-pulitzers-paywalls-and-investing-in-the-newsroom/.

———. 2015a. "Newsonomics: Razor-thin profits are cutting into newspapers' chances at innovation." Nieman Lab, May 14, 2015. Accessed March 25, 2016. http://www.niemanlab.org/2015/05/newsonomics-razor-thin-profits-are-cutting-into-newspapers-chances-at-innovation/.

———. 2015b. "Newsonomics: When news companies are no longer built to last." Nieman Lab, July 16, 2015. Accessed July 6, 2016. http://www.niemanlab.org/2015/07/newsonomics-when-news-companies-are-no-longer-built-to-last/.

———. 2016a. Newsonomics: The financialization of news is dimming the lights of the local press." Nieman Lab, February 19, 2016. Accessed March 31, 2017. http://www.niemanlab.org/2016/02/newsonomics-the-financialization-of-news-is-dimming-the-lights-of-the-local-press/.

———. 2016b. "Newsonomics: The New York Times reinvents Page One—and it's better than print ever was." Nieman Lab, March 7, 2016. Accessed August 17, 2018. http://www.niemanlab.org/2016/03/newsonomics-the-new-york-times-re-invents-page-one-and-its-better-than-print-ever-was/.

———. 2017a. "Newsonomics: The New York Times' Mark Thompson on regulating Facebook, global ambition, and when to stop the presses (forever)." Nieman Lab, November 13, 2017. Accessed August 15, 2018. http://www.niemanlab.org/2017/11/newsonomics-the-new-york-times-mark-thompson-on-regulating-facebook-global-ambition-and-when-to-stop-the-presses-forever.

———. 2017b. "Trump Bump grows into subscription surge—and not just for the New York Times." Nieman Lab, March 3, 2017. Accessed September 2, 2018. https://www.thestreet.com/story/14024114/1/trump-bump-grows-into-subscription-surge.html.

———. 2018. "Newsonomics: Alden Global Capital is making so much money wrecking local journalism it might not want to stop anytime soon." Nieman Lab, May 1, 2018. Accessed July 12, 2018. http://www.niemanlab.org/2018/05/newsonomics-alden-global-capital-is-making-so-much-money-wrecking-local-journalism-it-might-not-want-to-stop-anytime-soon/.

Domingo, David. 2008a. "Interactivity in the daily routines of online newsrooms: Dealing with an uncomfortable myth." *Journal of Computer-Mediated Communication* 13 (3): 680–704.

———. 2008b. "Inventing online journalism: A constructivist approach to the development of online news." In *Making online news: The ethnography of new media production*. Vol. 1, edited by Chris A. Paterson and David Domingo, 15–28. New York: Peter Lang.

Domingo, David, and Chris A. Paterson, eds. 2011. *Making online news: Newsroom ethnography in the second decade of Internet journalism*. Vol. 2. New York: Peter Lang.

Domingo, David, Thorsten Quandt, Ari Heinonen, Steve Paulussen, Jane B. Singer, and Marina Vujnovic. 2008. "Participatory journalism practices in the media and beyond: An international comparative study of initiatives in online newspapers." *Journalism Practice* 2 (3): 326–342.

Doyle, Gillian. 2013. "Re-invention and survival: Newspapers in the era of digital multiplatform delivery." *Journal of Media Business Studies* 10 (4): 1–20.

———. 2015. "Multi-platform media and the miracle of the loaves and fishes." *Journal of Media Business Studies* 12 (1): 49–65.

Economist, The. 2017. "Traditional media firms are enjoying a Trump bump." February 16, 2017. Accessed August 31, 2018. https://www.economist.com/business/2017/02/16/traditional-media-firms-are-enjoying-a-trump-bump.

Edge, Marc. 2014a. *Greatly exaggerated: The myth of the death of newspapers*. Vancouver, Canada: New Star Books.

———. 2014b. "Newspapers' annual reports show chains profitable." *Newspaper Research Journal* 35 (4): 66–82.

Edmonds, Rick. 2014a. "Advance digital makeover of its newspapers—five years in and no turning back." Poynter Institute, June 24, 2014. Accessed May 29, 2017. https://www.poynter.org/news/advance-digital-makeover-its-newspapers-five-years-and-no-turning-back.

———. 2014b. "Naysayers are swarming on Clayton Christensen and his 'gospel of innovation.'" Poynter Institute, June 19, 2014. Accessed April 14, 2017. https://www.poynter.org/2014/naysayers-are-swarming-on-clayton-christensen-and-his-gospel-of-innovation/255392/.

———. 2015. "Advance claims digital ad growth will outpace print declines in 2015." Poynter Institute, January 7, 2015. Accessed December 27, 2015. http://www.poynter.org/news/310555/advance-claims-digital-ad-growth-will-outpace-print-declines-in-2015/.

———. 2016a. "An ethical quandary for nonprofit journalism—are funders calling the shots?" Poynter Institute, April 20, 2016. Accessed August 16, 2018. https://www.poynter.org/news/ethical-quandary-nonprofit-journalism-are-funders-calling-shots.

———. 2016b. "Looking for a sustainable business model for a regional newspaper? Start at the Minneapolis Star Tribune." Poynter Institute, May 19, 2016. Accessed July 26, 2018. https://www.poynter.org/news/looking-sustainable-business-model-regional-newspaper-start-minneapolis-star-tribune.

———. 2016c. "Newspapers aren't dying as fast as you think." Poynter Institute, January 28, 2016. Accessed April 1, 2016. https://www.poynter.org/news/newspapers-arent-dying-fast-you-think.

———. 2018. "Why does the Star Tribune outperform the pack of metros? An update." Poynter Institute, May 2, 2018. Accessed August 20, 2018. https://www.poynter.org/news/why-does-star-tribune-outperform-pack-metros-update.

Ekdale, Brian, Melissa Tully, Shawn Harmsen, and Jane B. Singer. 2015. "Newswork within a culture of job insecurity: Producing news amidst organizational and industry uncertainty." *Journalism Practice* 9 (3): 383–398.

Ell, Kellie. 2018. "New York Times CEO: Print journalism has maybe another 10 years." CNBC, February 13, 2018. Accessed August 31, 2018. https://www.cnbc.com/2018/02/12/print-journalism-may-last-another-10-years-new-york-times-ceo.html.

Ember, Sydney. 2018. "New York Times Co. subscription revenue surpassed $1 billion in 2017." *New York Times,* February 8, 2018. Accessed August 10, 2018. https://www.nytimes.com/2018/02/08/business/new-york-times-company-earnings.html%20Accessed%20August%2010.

Enda, Jodi. 2006. "Blocked out: The Block family shutters its newspapers' Washington bureau." *American Journalism Review,* April/May 2006. Accessed March 27, 2018. http://ajrarchive.org/article.asp?id=4072.

Estrin, James. 2010. "If photojournalism is dead, what is Luceo?" *New York Times,* September 14, 2010. Accessed July 15, 2016. http://lens.blogs.nytimes.com/2010/09/14/if-photojournalism-is-dead-whats-luceo/.

Farhi, Paul. 2015. "In New Orleans, a journalistic experiment with unclear results." *Washington Post,* August 27, 2015. https://www.washingtonpost.com/lifestyle/style/in-new-orleans-a-journalistic-experiment-with-unclear-results/2015/08/27/d97f1500-4a85-11e5-8ab4-c73967a143d3_story.html?noredirect=on&utm_term=.70051897c276.

Fidler, Roger. 1997. *Mediamorphosis: Understanding new media.* Newbury Park, CA: Pine Forge Press.

Fink, James. 2018. "Buyouts leave deep cuts in Buffalo News staff, guild says." *Bizjournals,* June 13, 2018. Accessed September 14, 2018. https://www

.bizjournals.com/buffalo/news/2018/06/13/buyouts-leave-deep-cuts-in-buffalo-news-staff.html.

Fisher, Tyler. 2015. "Do visual stories make people care?" *National Public Radio*, November 15, 2015. Accessed December 19, 2017. http://blog.apps.npr.org/2015/11/19/sequential-visual-stories.html.

Fitzgerald, Mark. 2009. "Economist: Avista has only itself to blame in 'Strib' bankruptcy." *Editor and Publisher*, January 16, 2009. Accessed September 14, 2018. http://www.editorandpublisher.com/news/economist-avista-has-only-itself-to-blame-in-strib-bankruptcy/.

Frank, Laura. 2009. "The withering watchdog." PBS. Accessed March 5, 2017. http://www.pbs.org/wnet/expose/2009/06/the-withering-watchdog.html.

Fritz, Ben. 2010. "Most original news reporting comes from traditional sources, study finds." *Los Angeles Times*, January 11, 2010. Accessed July 24, 2016. http://articles.latimes.com/2010/jan/11/business/la-fi-ct-newspapers11-2010jan11.

Fuller, Melynda. 2018. "'Washington Post' to expand newsroom after second year of profits." Mediapost, January 9, 2018. Accessed August 12, 2018. https://www.mediapost.com/publications/article/312683/washington-post-to-expand-newsroom-after-second.html.

Fuoco, Michael. 2018a. "Controversy as *Pittsburgh Post-Gazette* newsroom confronts its publisher." *Columbia Journalism Review*, January 22, 2018. Accessed March 25, 2018. https://www.cjr.org/united_states_project/pittsburgh-post-gazette-newsroom-racist-editorial.php.

———. 2018b. "Newspaper Guild of Pittsburgh calls off successful four-day byline strike." Newspaper Guild of Pittsburgh, January 28, 2018. Accessed May 29, 2018. https://pghguild.com/2018/01/28/newspaper-guild-of-pittsburgh-calls-off-successful-four-day-byline-strike/.

Gade, Peter J., and Earnest L. Perry. 2003. "Changing the newsroom culture: A four-year case study of organizational development at the St. Louis Post-Dispatch." *Journalism and Mass Communication Quarterly* 80 (2): 327–347.

Gannon, Joyce. 2018. "Post-Gazette employees, newsroom editors emphasize they are separate from editorial pages." *Pittsburgh Post-Gazette*, June 19, 2018. Accessed June 19, 2018. http://www.post-gazette.com/business/pittsburgh-company-news/2018/06/19/Post-Gazette-employees-buy-ads-separate-from-editorial-pages-Rob-Rogers/stories/201806190023.

Garcia, Alex. 2013. "The idiocy of eliminating a photo staff." *Chicago Tribune*, May 30, 2013. Accessed July 15, 2016. http://newsblogs.chicagotribune.com/assignment-chicago/2013/05/the-idiocy-of-eliminating-a-photo-staff.html.

Garvin, Ben. 2014. "Pioneer Press photo staff to shoot exclusively with iPhones—April Fools!" twincities.com, April 1, 2014. Accessed September 1, 2014. http://blogs.twincities.com/flashgarvin/2014/04/01/pioneer-press-photo-staff-to-shoot-exclusively-with-iphones/.

Gillmor, Dan. 2006a. "The demise of the professional photojournalist." *Dan*

Gillmor (blog), December 4, 2006. Accessed October 23, 2008. http://citmedia.org/blog/2006/12/04/the-demise-of-the-professionalphoto journalist/.

———. 2006b. *We the media: Grassroots journalism by the people, for the people*. Sebastol, CA: O'Reilly Media.

———. 2009. "The decline (and maybe demise) of the professional photojournalist." *Dan Gillmor* (blog), December 2009. Accessed October 1, 2009. http://citmedia.org/blog/2006/12/04/the-demise-of-the-profes sionalphotojournalist/.

Grieco, Elizabeth. 2018. "Newsroom employment dropped nearly a quarter in less than 10 years, with greatest decline at newspapers." Pew Research Center, July 30, 2018. Accessed September 5, 2018. http://www.pewre search.org/fact-tank/2018/07/30/newsroom-employment-dropped-nearly-a-quarter-in-less-than-10-years-with-greatest-decline-at-news papers/.

Griggs, Ted. 2015. "The Advocate Overtakes the Times Picayune as Louisiana's Largest Newspaper." theadvocate.com, January 27, 2015. Accessed February 26, 2016. https://www.theadvocate.com/baton_rouge/news/business/article_4c9e155e-4694-5281-a479-3312ff28ab28.html.

GroundTruth Project. 2019. "New initiative: Report for America." Accessed July 26, 2019. https://thegroundtruthproject.org/projects/report-for-america/.

Gyllenhaal, Anders, and Moses, Monica. 2006. "A newspaper's redesign signals its renewal." Nieman Lab, March 15, 2006. Accessed February 12, 2018. http://niemanreports.org/articles/a-newspapers-redesign-signals-its-renewal/.

Hamm, Kevin. 2013a. "Digital first: A look at Advance Publications' strategy." Denver Newspaper Guild, June 28, 2013. Accessed May 14, 2017. http://denvernewspaperguild.org/digital-first-a-look-at-advance-publi cations-strategy/.

———. 2013b. "Unions: Journal Register Co. has 'declared war.'" Denver Newspaper Guild, March 6, 2013. Accessed June 8, 2017. http://den vernewspaperguild.org/unions-journal-register-co-has-declared-war/.

Hare, Kristen. 2016. "At the Minneapolis Star Tribune, a newsroom that's gone from surviving to thriving." Poynter Institute, November 2, 2016. Accessed May 4, 2018. https://www.poynter.org/news/minneapolis-star-tribune-newsroom-thats-gone-surviving-thriving.

———. 2017a. "How The Minneapolis Star Tribune covered the death of a plucky community hero." Poynter Institute, January 26, 2017. Accessed January 10, 2019. https://www.poynter.org/reporting-editing/2017/how-the-minneapolis-star-tribune-covered-the-death-of-a-plucky-commu nity-hero/.

———. 2017b. "In Philadelphia, 3 newsrooms had to become 1. Now, they're taking on a whole new kind of change." Poynter Institute, May 18, 2017. Accessed November 28, 2017. https://www.poynter.org/news/philadelphia-3-newsrooms-had-become-1-now-theyre-taking-whole-new-kind-change.

Hermida, Alfred, David Domingo, Ari Heinonen, Steve Paulussen, Thorsten Quandt, Zvi Reich, Jane B. Singer, and Marina Vujnovic. 2011. "The active recipient: Participatory journalism through the lens of the Dewey-Lippmann debate." *International Symposium on Online Journalism* 1 (2). https://biblio.ugent.be/publication/1202253/file/1202278.

Hermida, Alfred, and Neil Thurman. 2008. "A clash of cultures: The integration of user-generated content within professional journalistic frameworks at British newspaper websites." *Journalism Practice* 2 (3): 343–356.

Holmqvist, Kenneth, Jana Holsanova, Mari Barthelson, and Daniel Lundqvist. 2003. "Reading or scanning? A study of newspaper and net paper reading." *Mind* 2 (3): 657–670.

Horton, Brian. 2001. *The Associated Press guide to photojournalism.* New York: McGraw-Hill.

Huffaker, Sandy. 2013. "Photojournalism is not dead." *Sandy Huffaker,* September 4, 2013. Accessed July 15, 2016. http://sandyhuffakerjr.blogspot.com/2013/09/blog-post.html.

Hutchins, Corey. 2016. "Fearing job cuts, Denver Post journalists rally against their hedge fund owner." *Colorado Independent,* June 17, 2016. Accessed June 8, 2017. https://www.coloradoindependent.com/2016/06/17/denver-post-rally-buyouts/.

———. 2018. "Meet the journalist tracking Digital First Media's hedge fund owner." *Columbia Journalism Review,* March 29, 2018. Accessed July 12, 2018. https://www.cjr.org/united_states_project/digital-first-alden-newsmatters.php.

Irby, Kenny. 2002. "Why photojournalism matters." Poynter Institute, November 4, 2002. Accessed July 15, 2016.http://www.poynter.org/2002/why-photojournalism-matters/3334/.

———. 2013. "John White on Sun-Times layoffs: 'It was as if they pushed a button and deleted a whole culture.'" Poynter Institute, May 31, 2013. Accessed July 15, 2016. http://www.poynter.org/news/mediawire/215016/john-white-on-sun-times-layoffs-it-was-as-if-they-pushed-a-button-and-deleted-a-whole-culture/.

Jenkins, Henry. 2006. *Convergence culture: Where old and new media collide.* New York: New York University Press.

Jolly, David. 2009. "Lament for a dying field: Photojournalism." *New York Times,* August 9, 2009. Accessed July 15, 2016. https://www.newytimes.com/2009/08/10/business/media/10photo.html?pagewanted=all&_r=0.

Kirkland, Sam. 2014. "One year after 28 Sun-Times photojournalists were laid off, where are they now?" Poynter Institute, May 30, 2014. Accessed July 20, 2016. https://www.poynter.org/latest-news/mediawire/254014/one-year-after-28-sun-times-photojournalists-were-laid-off-where-are-they-now.

Kitschke, Zach. 2017. "Why visual communication is the most important skill for journalists in 2015." *Huffington Post,* December 6, 2017. Accessed December 19, 2017. https://www.huffingtonpost.com/zach-kitschke/post_9445_b_7456664.html.

Klein, Christopher. 2017. "What was the census war?" *History,* March 29, 2017. Accessed July 8, 2018. https://www.history.com/news/what-was-the-census-war.

Klein-Avraham, Inbal, and Zvi Reich. 2016. "Out of the frame: A longitudinal perspective on digitization and professional photojournalism." *New Media and Society* 18 (3): 429–446.

Knight Foundation. 2011. "Getting local: How nonprofit news ventures seek sustainability." October 2011. Accessed July 12, 2018. https://www.knightfoundation.org/media/uploads/publication_pdfs/13664_KF_NPNews_Overview_10-17-2.pdf.

———. 2013. "Finding a foothold: How nonprofit news ventures seek sustainability." October 29, 2013. Accessed July 12, 2018. https://knightfoundation.org/reports/finding-foothold.

———. 2017. "Digital transformation of local news organizations focus of new $4.8 million investment from Knight Foundation and the Lenfest Institute for Journalism." February 13. Accessed July 12, 2018.https://knightfoundation.org/press/releases/digital-transformation-of-local-news-organizations-focus-of-new-4-8-million-investment-from-knight-foundation-and-the-lenfest-institute-for-journalism.

Kobre, Ken. 2004. *Photojournalism: The professionals' approach.* Boston: Focal Press.

Konieczna, Magda. 2014. "Do old norms have a place in new media? A case study of the nonprofit MinnPost." *Journalism Practice* 8 (1): 49–64.

Kurtz, Howard. 2009. "Rocky Mountain News to cease publication." *Washington Post,* February 27, 2009. Accessed July 22, 2016. http://www.washingtonpost.com/wp-dyn/content/article/2009/02/26/AR2009022602108.html.

Kuttner, Robert, and Hildy Zenger. 2017. "Saving the free press from private equity." *Prospect,* December 27, 2017. Accessed July 26, 2018. http://prospect.org/article/saving-free-press-private-equity.

Lacy, Stephen, Michael Stamm, and Hugh Martin. 2014. "Short-run decisions threaten papers' long-run viability." *Newspaper Research Journal* 35 (4): 6–20.

Lakshmanan, Indira. 2018. "Abomination": Pittsburgh publisher's editorial inflames newsroom, readers." Poynter Institute, January 19, 2018. Accessed March 27, 2018. https://www.poynter.org/news/abomination-pittsburgh-publishers-editorial-inflames-newsroom-readers.

Langton, Loup. 2008. *Photojournalism and today's news.* West Sussex, UK: Wiley-Blackwell.

Lee, Deron. 2017. "The pleasure and pain of going nonprofit." *Columbia Journalism Review,* Spring 2017. Accessed August 17, 2018. https://www.cjr.org/local_news/nonprofit-news-local-tulsa-frontier.php.

Lee-Wright, Peter, Angela Phillips, and Tamara Witschge. 2011. *Changing journalism.* New York: Routledge.

Lenfest Institute. 2017. "Lenfest Institute for Journalism launches $1 million in local news and innovation grants, entrepreneur in residence program." June 5, 2017. Accessed July 12, 2018. https://www.lenfestinstitute.org/news-posts/lenfest-institute-journalism-launches-1-million-local-news-information-innovation-grants-entrepreneur-residence-program/.

———. n.d. "About Us." Accessed August 17, 2018. https://www.lenfestinstitute.org/about/.

Lewis, Seth C., Kelly Kaufhold, and Dominic L. Lasorsa. 2010. "Thinking about citizen journalism: The philosophical and practical challenges of user-generated content for community newspapers." *Journalism Practice* 4 (2): 163–179.

Lichterman, Joseph. 2017. "The Washington Post is putting big bet on video (and trying to break into Daily Show–style comedy)." Nieman Lab, January 17, 2017. Accessed December 19, 2017. http://www.niemanlab.org/2017/01/the-washington-post-is-putting-a-big-bet-on-video-and-trying-to-break-into-daily-show-style-comedy/.

Lindstrom, Natasha. 2018. "Pittsburgh Post-Gazette to stop publishing in print two days a week." triblive.com, June 27, 2018. Accessed December 19, 2018. https://triblive.com/local/allegheny/13809455-74/pittsburgh-post-gazette-to-stop-publishing-in-print-two-days-a-week.

Lischka, Juliane A. 2015. "How structural multi-platform newsroom features and innovative values alter journalistic cross-channel and cross-sectional working procedures." *Journal of Media Business Studies* 12 (1): 7–28.

Lisheron, Mark. 2012. "On the rebound." *American Journalism Review*, August/September 2012. Accessed July 26, 2018. http://ajrarchive.org/article.asp?id=5390.

Lowrey, Wilson. 2002. "Word people vs. picture people: Normative differences and strategies for control over work among newsroom subgroups." *Mass Communication and Society* 5 (4): 411–432.

Lyons, Kim. 2018a. "In Pittsburgh, an unprecedented blow to editorial cartoonist." *Columbia Journalism Review*, June 11, 2018. Accessed June 13, 2018. https://www.cjr.org/united_states_project/post-gazette-rob-rogers-cartoons.php.

———. 2018b. "The Pittsburgh *Post-Gazette*'s baffling editorial decision." *Columbia Journalism Review*, March 22, 2018. Accessed March 23, 2018. https://www.cjr.org/united_states_project/burris-block-racism-editorial.php.

Ma, Adrian. 2018. "Plain Dealer plans to lay off a third of unionized news staff." Ideastream, December 17, 2018. Accessed January 2, 2019. https://www.ideastream.org/news/plain-dealer-plans-to-lay-off-a-third-of-unionized-news-staff.

Mäenpää, Jenni. 2014. "Rethinking photojournalism: The changing work practices and professionalism of photojournalists in the digital age." *Nordicom Review* 35 (2): 91–104.

McIntyre, Douglas A. 2009. "The 10 most endangered newspapers in America." *Time*, March 9, 2009. http://content.time.com/time/business/article/0,8599,1883785-1,00.html.

McQuaid, John. 2012. "Why a weak website can't replace a daily newspaper in New Orleans." *The Atlantic,* June 12, 2012. Accessed May 14, 2017. https://www.theatlantic.com/national/archive/2012/06/why-a-weak-website-cant-replace-a-daily-newspaper-in-new-orleans/258393/.

Media Insight Project. 2018. "Appendix 1: Respondents' demographics and news behaviors." American Press Institute. Accessed August 20, 2018. https://www.americanpressinstitute.org/publications/reports/survey-research/subscribers-appendix-1/.

Meryhew, Richard. 2013. "Star Tribune wins two Pulitzer Prizes." *Star Tribune,* April 16, 2013. Accessed July 26, 2018. http://www.startribune.com/star-tribune-wins-two-pulitzer-prizes/203068551/.

Meyer, Philip. 1995. "Learning to love lower profits." *American Journalism Review,* December 1995. Accessed March 25, 2016. http://www.unc.edu/~pmeyer/ajrprofits/profits1.html.

———. 2009. *The vanishing newspaper: Saving journalism in the information age.* Columbia: University of Missouri Press.

Miles, Robert P. 2002. *Warren Buffett CEO: Secrets from the Berkshire Hathaway managers.* New York: John Wiley and Sons.

Miller, Jay. 2013. "*Plain Dealer* says print reduction is driven by digital." *Crain's Cleveland Business,* April 15, 2013. Accessed June 5, 2017. http://www.crainscleveland.com/article/20130415/SUB1/304159965/plain-dealer.

———. 2014. "One year later: checking in with the Northeast Ohio Media Group." *Crain's Cleveland Business,* August 25, 2014. Accessed December 1, 2015. http://www.crainscleveland.com/article/20140824/SUB1/308249980/one-year-later-checking-in-with-the-northeast-ohio-media-group.

Minnesota News Guild. 2014. "Wanted: New owners at the St. Paul Pioneer Press and other DFM papers." September 7, 2014. Accessed July 13, 2018. http://www.mnguild.org/wanted-new-owners-st-paul-pioneer-press-dfm-papers/.

Mitchell, Amy, and Jesse Holcomb. 2016. "State of the news media, 2016." Pew Research Center's Journalism Project, June 15, 2016. Accessed June 16, 2016. http://www.journalism.org/2014/03/26/state-of-the-news-media-2014-overview/.

Mitchell, Dan. 2013. "Chicago Sun Times fires its entire photo staff." *Fortune,* May 31, 2013. Accessed July 20, 2016. http://fortune.com/2013/05/31/chicago-sun-times-fires-its-entire-photo-staff/.

Monaghan, Garrett, and Sean Tunney. 2010. *Web journalism: A new form of citizenship?* Eastbourne East Sussex, UK: Sussex Academic Press.

Montgomery, Robb. 2017. "Visual-first journalism at The New York Times (and everywhere)." World Association of Newspapers and News Publishers, January 19, 2017. Accessed January 12, 2018. https://blog.wan-ifra.org/2017/01/19/visual-first-journalism-at-the-new-york-times-and-everywhere.

Mortensen, Tara Buehner, and Ana Keshelashvili. 2013. "If everyone with a camera can do this, then what? Professional photojournalists' sense of professional threat in the face of citizen photojournalism." *Visual Communication Quarterly* 20 (3): 144–158.

Mortensen, Tara Marie. 2014. "Blurry and centered or clear and balanced? Citizen photojournalists and professional photojournalists' understanding of each other's visual values." *Journalism Practice* 8 (6): 704–725.

Moses, Monica. 2002. "The elements of powerful pages." Poynter Institute, August 13, 2002. Accessed December 19, 2017. https://www.poynter.org/news/elements-powerful-pages.

Mullen, Mike. 2016a. "The plot to save the Pioneer Press from its hedge fund owners." *City Pages*, May 4, 2016. Accessed July 3, 2018. http://www.citypages.com/news/the-plot-to-save-the-pioneer-press-from-its-hedge-fund-owners-8249721.

———. 2016b. "Star Tribune owner Glen Taylor: I'd buy the PiPress, but the Justice Department has no chill." *City Pages*, October 19, 2016. Accessed July 22, 2018. http://www.citypages.com/news/star-tribune-owner-glen-taylor-id-buy-the-pipress-but-the-justice-department-has-no-chill/397592031.

Murray, Susan. 2008. "Digital images, photo-sharing, and our shifting notions of everyday aesthetics." *Journal of Visual Culture* 7 (2): 147–163.

Myers, Steve. 2012. "Digital First Media CEO likes Times-Picayune's new digital-first model." Poynter Institute, July 11, 2012. Accessed May 14, 2017. https://www.poynter.org/2012/digital-first-media-ceo-likes-times-picayunes-new-digital-first-model/180650/.

National Press Photographers Association. 2008. "Cut Newsday photographers told to 're-apply for visual journalist jobs.'" December 8, 2008. Accessed July 21, 2016. https://nppa.org/news/1123.

———. 2014. "Photo upheaval at Orlando Sentinel." February 27, 2014. Accessed July 15, 2016. https://nppa.org/news/photo-upheaval-orlando-sentinel.

New Orleans Magazine. 2016. "The T-P and The Advocate: Four years later." November 2016. Accessed May 11, 2017. http://www.myneworleans.com/New-Orleans-Magazine/November-2016/The-T-P-and-The-Advocate/.

NewsGuild. 2018. "Rebellion builds at Alden-owned newspapers." May 17, 2018. Accessed July 13, 2018. http://www.newsguild.org/mediaguild3/rebellion-builds-at-alden-owned-newspapers/.

Nielsen Norman Group. 2010. "Photos as web content." November 1, 2010. Accessed July 15, 2016. https://www.nngroup.com/articles/photos-as-web-content/.

Oliphant, Grant, and Maxwell King. 2018. "Shame." Pittsburgh Foundation/Heinz Endowments, January 15, 2018. Accessed March 25, 2018. http://www.heinz.org/just-pittsburgh/shame.

O'Sullivan, John, and Ari Heinonen. 2008. "Old values, new media: Journalism role perceptions in a changing world." *Journalism Practice* 2 (3): 357–371.

Painter, Kristen Leigh. 2015. "Star Tribune reshapes itself for future with move to new offices." *Star Tribune*, March 20, 2015. Accessed July 27,

2018. http://m.startribune.com/star-tribune-reshapes-itself-for-future-with-move-to-new-offices/296916681/.

Pantti, Mervi. 2013. "Getting closer? Encounters of the national media with global images." *Journalism Studies* 14 (2): 201–218.

Pantti, Mervi, and Piet Bakker. 2009. "Misfortunes, memories and sunsets: Non-professional images in Dutch news media." *International Journal of Cultural Studies* 12 (5): 471–489.

Paterson, Chris A. 2011. "Convergence in the news wholesalers: Trends in international news agencies." In *Making online news*. Vol. 2, edited by David Domingo and Chris A. Paterson, 129–139. New York: Peter Lang.

Paterson, Chris A., and David Domingo, eds. 2008. *Making online news: The ethnography of new media production*. Vol. 1. New York: Peter Lang.

Paulussen, Steve, and Pieter Ugille. 2008. "User generated content in the newsroom: Professional and organisational constraints on participatory journalism." *Westminster Papers in Communication and Culture* 5 (2). http://citeseerx.ist.psu.edu/viewdoc/download?doi=10.1.1.459.8314&rep=rep1&type=pdf.

Perez-Pena, Richard. 2009. "Rocky Mountain News fails to find a buyer and will close." *New York Times,* February 26, 2009. Accessed July 22, 2016. http://www.nytimes.com/2009/02/27/business/media/27paper.html?_r=0.

Pew Research Center. 2010. "How news happens." January 11, 2010. Accessed May 3, 2017. http://www.journalism.org/2010/01/11/how-news-happens/.

———. 2018. "Newspaper fact sheet." June 13, 2018. Accessed September 9, 2018. http://www.journalism.org/fact-sheet/newspapers/.

PG NewsSlide. 2019. "A new multimedia news medium." Accessed January 4, 2019. https://pgnewsslide.com/.

Phelps, David. 2009. "Star Tribune files for Chapter 11 bankruptcy." *Star Tribune,* January 16, 2009. Accessed July 8, 2018. http://www.startribune.com/star-tribune-files-for-chapter-11-bankruptcy/37685134/.

Phillips, Angela. 2014. *Journalism in context: Practice and theory for the digital age*. New York: Routledge.

Pink, Sarah. 2011. "Amateur photographic practice, collective representation and the constitution of place." *Visual Studies* 26 (2): 92–101.

Pittsburgh Post-Gazette. 2014. "Building for the Future." Paper presented to the International Newspaper Group, February 4, 2014. Accessed October 20, 2017. http://internationalnewspapergroup.org/wp-content/uploads/2015/10/Lisa-Hurm-Pittsburg-Post-Gazette-Update.pdf.

———. 2018. "Editorial director for Block newspapers named." *Pittsburgh Post-Gazette,* March 2, 2018. Accessed March 27, 2018. http://www.post-gazette.com/business/career-workplace/2018/03/02/Editorial-director-for-Block-newspapers-named/stories/201803020188.

PublicSource. 2018. "In-depth stories for a better Pittsburgh." Accessed May 30, 2018. https://www.publicsource.org.

Quinn, Chris. 2016. "We made a big mistake over the weekend and we should not have." cleveland.com, April 11, 2016. Accessed July 28, 2016. http://

www.cleveland.com/metro/index.ssf/2016/04/we_made_a_big_mistake_over_the.html.

Quinn, Sara. 2007. "Looking back at eyetrack: Poynter's history of studying reader habits." Poynter Institute, March 14, 2007. Accessed July 20, 2016. http://www.poynter.org/2007/looking-back-at-eyetrack-poynters-history-of-studying-reader-habits/81253/.

———. 2015. "Eyetracking photojournalism: New research explores what makes a photograph memorable, shareable, and worth publishing." *News Photographer*, January 27, 2015. Accessed July 22, 2016. https://nppa.org/eyetracking-photojournalism-new-research-explores-what-makes-photograph-memorable-shareable-and-worth-publishing.

Real Clear Politics. 2014. "The Top 10 Newspapers in Trouble." March 17, 2014. Accessed July 22, 2016. http://www.realclearpolitics.com/lists/top_10_newspapers_in_trouble/st_paul_pioneer_press.html?state=play.

Reference for Business. 2018. "Block Communications, Inc." Accessed April 12, 2018. https://www.referenceforbusiness.com/history2/17/Block-Communications-Inc.html.

Reinardy, Scott. 2016. *Journalism's lost generation: The un-doing of US newspaper newsrooms*. New York: Routledge.

Reynolds, Julie. 2018a. "Alden Global's desperate crackdown." DFM Workers, April 27, 2018. Accessed July 11, 2018. https://dfmworkers.org/alden-globals-desperate-crackdown/.

———. 2018b. "Hedge fund Alden siphoned 100s of millions from newspapers in scheme to gamble on other investments, suit says." DFM Workers, March 8, 2018. Accessed July 13, 2018. https://dfmworkers.org/hedge-fund-alden-siphoned-100s-of-millions-from-newspapers-in-scheme-to-gamble-on-other-investments-suit-says/.

Rieder, Rem. 2014. "The embattled newspaper business." *USA Today*, October 1, 2014. Accessed March 25, 2016. http://www.usatoday.com/story/money/columnist/rieder/2014/10/01/more-newspaper-layoffs/16531733/.

———. 2016a. "Rieder: Battered newspapers still important." *USA Today*, January 13, 2016. Accessed February 26, 2016. http://www.usatoday.com/story/money/columnist/rieder/2016/01/13/rieder-battered-and-beleaguered-newspapers-remain-important/78736456/.

———. 2016b. "Rieder: Newspapers haven't 'cracked code,' Buffett says." *USA Today*, May 25, 2016. Accessed August 11, 2017. https://www.usatoday.com/story/money/columnist/rieder/2016/05/25/rieder-newspapers-havent-cracked-code-buffett-says/84902818/.

———. 2017. "Endowment to support Philadelphia media on track to exceed $100M." *Columbia Journalism Review*, May 3, 2017. Accessed August 18, 2018. https://www.cjr.org/business_of_news/philadelphia-news-philanthropy-lenfest.php.

Ritchin, Fred. 2013. *Bending the frame*. New York: Aperture.

Robinson, Sue. 2011. "Convergence crises: News work and news space in the digitally transforming newsroom." *Journal of Communication* 61 (6): 1122–1141.

Robson, Britt. 2014. "Glen Taylor: How I bought the Star Tribune and what I paid." *MinnPost,* April 17, 2014. Accessed July 27, 2018. https://www.minnpost.com/business/2014/04/glen-taylor-how-i-bought-star-tribune-and-what-i-paid/.

Rodrigue, George. 2015. "Reporting on problems with solutions in mind: George Rodrigue." cleveland.com, September 19, 2015. Accessed January 7, 2016. http://www.cleveland.com/metro/index.ssf/2015/09/reporting_on_problems_with_sol.html.

Rogers, Rob. 2018. "I was fired for making fun of Trump." *New York Times,* June 15, 2018. Accessed June 18, 2018. https://www.nytimes.com/2018/06/15/opinion/cartoonist-rob-rogers-trump-fired.html.

Romano, Aja. 2013. "Tumblr documents the Chicago Sun-Times' descent into iPhone photography." Daily Dot, July 3, 2013. Accessed July 21, 2016. https://www.dailydot.com/irl/tumblr-sun-times-dark-times-photojournalism-iphone/.

Romenesko, Jim. 2014. "Plain Dealer ombud: Why I haven't written about the editorial board video brouhaha." *Jim Romenesko,* November 4, 2014. Accessed January 29, 2016. http://jimromenesko.com/2014/11/04/plain-dealer-ombud-why-i-havent-written-about-the-campaign-video-removal-controversy/.

Romero, Dennis. 2011. "Newspapers dead within five years, USC predicts." laweekly.com, December 14, 2011. Accessed February 26, 2016. http://www.laweekly.com/news/newspapers-dead-within-five-years-usc-predicts-2395696.

Ryfe, David. 2012. *Can journalism survive? An inside look at American newsrooms.* Hoboken, NJ: John Wiley and Sons.

Sambrook, Richard. 2017. "Stop press? Last words on the future of newspapers." *The Conversation,* January 31, 2017. Accessed September 5, 2018. http://theconversation.com/stop-press-last-words-on-the-future-of-newspapers-72027.

Sandy, Eric. 2013. "The Northeast Ohio Media Group is hiring for all the positions that were literally just cut." Cleveland Scene, July 17, 2013. Accessed December 23, 2015. http://www.clevescene.com/cleveland/the-northeast-ohio-media-group-is-hiring-for-all-the-positions-that-were-literally-just-cut/Content?oid=3608227.

Schizer, David M. 2011. "Subsidizing the press: It is time for news organizations to begin making greater use of the nonprofit form." *Columbia Law School Magazine,* August 19, 2011. Accessed March 31, 2016. https://docplayer.net/52625076-Fromthe-dean-on-august-19-david-m-schizer-dean-and-the-lucy-g-moses-professor-of-law-welcomed.html.

Serafinelli, Elisa. 2017. "Analysis of photo sharing and visual social relationships: Instagram as a case study." *Photographies* 10 (1): 91–111.

Shafer, Jack. 2016. "What if the newspaper industry made a colossal mistake?" *Politico Magazine,* October 17, 2016. Accessed May 9, 2017. http://www.politico.com/magazine/story/2016/10/newspapers-digital-first-214363.

Shapiro, Michael, Anna Hiatt, and Mike Hoyt. 2015. *Tales from the great disruption: Insights and lessons from journalism's technological transformation.* Highland Park, IL: Big Roundtable Books.

Sheehan, Andy. 2018. "Post-Gazette's endorsement of Rick Saccone surprises many, angers some." CBS, March 12, 2018. Accessed March 27, 2018. http://pittsburgh.cbslocal.com/2018/03/12/post-gazette-rick-saccone-endorsement/.

Shister, Gail. 2010. "The shot heard 'round the industry: Backpack journalism on the rise." adweek.com, February 26, 2010. Accessed December 22, 2017. http://www.adweek.com/tvnewser/the-shot-heard-round-the-industry-backpack-journalism-on-the-rise/26372.

Singer, Jane B. 2004. "More than ink-stained wretches: The resocialization of print journalists in converged newsrooms." *Journalism and Mass Communication Quarterly* 81 (4): 838–856.

Singer, Jane B., David Domingo, Ari Heinonen, Alfred Hermida, Steve Paulussen, Thorsten Quandt, Zvi Reich, and Marina Vujnovic. 2011. *Participatory journalism: Guarding open gates at online newspapers.* Hoboken, NJ: John Wiley and Sons.

Smith, Allan. 2018. "People are furious with Pittsburgh's 'liberal' newspaper after it endorsed the Trump-backed Republican in the nation's biggest election." AOL, March 12, 2018. Accessed March 27, 2018. https://www.aol.com/article/news/2018/03/12/people-are-furious-with-pittsburghs-liberal-newspaper-after-it-endorsed-the-trump-backed-republican-in-the-nations-biggest-election/23383786/.

Sommer, Mark. 2016. "Q&A: Newsguild president Bernie Lunzer." Buffalo Newspaper Guild, May 12, 2016. Accessed August 23, 2017. http://www.buffaloguild.org/2016/05/12/qa-newsguild-president-bernie-lunzer/.

Sonderman, Jeff. 2011. "Most print newspapers have 5 years to live, USC report claims." Poynter Institute, December 15, 2011. Accessed February 26, 2016. http://www.poynter.org/2011/most-print-newspapers-have-5-years-to-live-usc-report-claims/156197/. (The 2011 article was updated and revised in 2015.)

Spears, Jared. 2018. "Pursuing 'subscriber-first' strategy, The New York Times learns to think like a consumer brand." State of Digital Publishing, May 10, 2018. Accessed September 8, 2018. https://www.stateofdigitalpublishing.com/opinion/pursuing-subscriber-first-strategy-york-times-learns-consumer-brand/.

Spinner, Jackie. 2013. "'Identity crisis' in photojournalism." *American Journalism Review,* December 4, 2013. Accessed November 2, 2014. http://ajr.org/2013/12/04/photojurnalism-new-era/.

Starkman, Dean. 2014. *The watchdog that didn't bark: The financial crisis and the disappearance of investigative journalism.* New York: Columbia University Press.

Sterling, Christopher. H., ed. 2009. *Encyclopedia of journalism.* Thousand Oaks, CA: Sage Publications.

Sterling, Ellen. 2011. "Digital first: What does it mean, and where will it take us?" *Editor and Publisher,* December 13, 2011. Accessed June 5, 2017. http://www.editorandpublisher.com/feature/digital-first-what-does-it-mean-and-where-will-it-take-us/.

Sterne, Peter. 2013. "The Newspaper Guild on the Cleveland *Plain Dealer* layoffs." Observer Innovation, August 2, 2013. Accessed November 19, 2015. http://observer.com/2013/08/cleveland-plain-dealer-lays-off-nearly-50-journalists/.

Stevens, Jane. 2002. "Backpack journalism is here to stay." *Online Journalism Review,* April 2, 2002. Accessed December 22, 2017. http://www.ojr.org/ojr/workplace/1017771575.php.

Stone, Martha. 2002. "The backpack journalist is a 'mush of mediocrity.'" *Online Journalism Review,* April 2, 2002. Accessed December 22, 2017. http://www.ojr.org/ojr/workplace/1017771634.php.

Sullivan, Margaret. 2018a. "As papers dwindle, local news is hit hard." *Washington Post,* August 6, 2018, C1.

———. 2018b. "Is this strip-mining or journalism? 'Sobs, gasps, expletives' over latest Denver Post layoffs." *Washington Post,* March 15, 2018. Accessed July 11, 2018. https://www.washingtonpost.com/lifestyle/style/is-this-strip-mining-or-journalism-sobs-gasps-expletives-over-latest-denver-post-layoffs/2018/03/15/d05abc5a-287e-11e8-874b-d517e912f125_story.html?utm_term=.c840c5f5e46e.

Taylor, Glen. 2014. "Glen Taylor: Why I bought Star Tribune; what I see for its future." *Star Tribune,* July 6, 2014. Accessed July 27, 2018. http://www.startribune.com/glen-taylor-why-i-bought-star-tribune-what-i-see-for-its-future/265754881/.

Temple, John. 2009. "Lessons from the Rocky Mountain News—Text and video of speech delivered at UC Berkeley Media Technology Summit at Google in Silicon Valley." *Temple Talk* (blog), September 30, 2009. Accessed July 19, 2019. http://www.johntemple.net/2009/09/lessons-from-rocky-mountain-news-text.html.

Theim, Rebecca. 2013a. "Good til the last drop: The future of Advance Publications and The Plain Dealer in the wake of 'digital-first' media." Clevescene, October 23, 2013. Accessed December 1, 2015. http://www.clevescene.com/cleveland/the-future-of-advance-publications-and-the-plain-dealer-in-the-wake-of-digital-first-media/Content?oid=3684399.

———. 2013b. *Hell and high water: The battle to save the daily "New Orleans Times-Picayune."* Gretna, LA: Pelican Publishing.

———. 2013c. "Holding the Newhouses to 'The Pledge': A newspaper's ex-employees sue over an abandoned "no-layoffs" promise." *Columbia Journalism Review,* December 24, 2013. Accessed December 1, 2015. http://www.cjr.org/the_audit/holding_the_newhouses_to_the_p.php.

———. 2015. "The Internet didn't doom the daily New Orleans Times-Picayune; Katrina did." Jstordaily.org, August 21, 2015. Accessed May 16, 2017. https://daily.jstor.org/times-picayune-after-katrina/.

Trickey, Erick. 2013. "Plain Dealer going to 3-day home delivery, 7-day newsstand edition." *Cleveland Magazine,* April 4, 2013. Accessed June

5, 2017. http://clevelandmagazine.blogspot.com/2013/04/plain-dealer-going-to-3-day-home.html.

Ulloa, Luis Carcamo, Mari-Carmen Mora, Ramon Cladellas Pros, and Antoni Castello Tarrida. 2015. "News photography for Facebook: Effects of images on the visual behaviour of readers in three simulated newspaper formats." *Information Research* 20 (1): 315–333.

Uren, Adam. 2018. "Inside the hedge fund–owned Pioneer Press newsroom, frustration reigns." Bring Me the News, May 4. Accessed July 6, 2018. https://bringmethenews.com/minnesota-news/inside-the-hedge-fund-owned-pioneer-press-newsroom-frustration-reigns.

Usher, Nikki. 2013. "When newsrooms move newsrooms, is it about decline or about digital?" Nieman Lab, November 5, 2013. Accessed December 6, 2017. http://www.niemanlab.org/2013/11/when-newsrooms-move-newsrooms-is-it-about-decline-or-about-digital/.

———. 2014a. *Making news at* The New York Times. Ann Arbor: University of Michigan Press.

———. 2014b. "Moving the newsroom: Post-industrial news spaces and places." Columbia University Academic Commons, 1–61. Accessed December 29, 2017. https://academiccommons.columbia.edu/doi/10.7916/D8CJ8RRZ.

———. 2015. "Newsroom moves and the newspaper crisis evaluated: Space, place, and cultural meaning." *Media, Culture and Society* 37 (7): 1005–1021.

Van House, Nancy A. 2011. "Personal photography, digital technologies and the uses of the visual." *Visual Studies* 26 (2): 125–134.

Villi, Mikko, and Matteo Stocchetti. 2011. "Visual mobile communication, mediated presence and the politics of space." *Visual Studies* 26 (2): 102–112.

Waldman, Steven. 2011. *Information needs of communities: The changing media landscape in a broadband age.* Collingdale, PA: Diane Publishing.

Walker, David. 2012. "An eye-tracking study delivers eye-grabbing conclusions." Shorewalker, January 18, 2012. Accessed, July 20, 2016. http://shorewalker.com/archive/section-1/eyetrack-poynter.html.

———. 2014. "New York Daily News lays off nine photo staffers, including David Handschuh." PDN Pulse, July 21, 2014. Accessed July 15, 2016. http://pdnpulse.pdnonline.com/2014/07/new-york-daily-news-lays-nine-photo-staffers-including-david-handschuh.html.

Walters, Natalie. 2017. "This timeline of layoffs and buyouts at the New York Times shows why the staff is staging a walkout." TheStreet, June 29, 2017. Accessed August 15, 2018. https://www.thestreet.com/story/14204771/1/this-timeline-of-layoffs-and-buyouts-at-the-new-york-times-shows-why-the-staff-is-angry.html.

Wang, Shan. 2016. "A changing of the guard at nonprofit MinnPost, a bright spot in sustainable, online local news." Nieman Lab, October 18, 2016. Accessed August 24, 2018. http://www.niemanlab.org/2016/10/a-changing-of-the-guard-at-nonprofit minnpost-a-bright-spot-in-sustainable-online-local-news/.

Washeck, Angela. 2014. What newsroom spaces tell us about the future of digital journalism." MediaShift, May 19, 2014. Accessed December 28, 2017. http://mediashift.org/2014/05/what-newsroom-spaces-tell-us-about-the-future-of-digital-journalism/.

White, Jaquetta. 2012. "*Times-Picayune* lays off nearly one-third of its staff." nola.com, June 12, 2012. Accessed April 20, 2017. http://www.nola.com/business/index.ssf/2012/06/times-picayune_employees_to_le.html.

Wingerd, Mary. 2007. "Separated at birth: The sibling rivalry of Minneapolis and St. Paul." Organization of American Historians, February 2007. Accessed June 15, 2018. http://www.oah.org/pubs/nl/2007feb/wingerd.html.

Winslow, Donald, 2013. "Chicago Sun-Times wipes out photo staff." National Press Photographers Association, May 30, 2013. Accessed July 15, 2016. https://nppa.org/news/chicago-sun-times-wipes-out-photo-staff.

Witschge, Tamara, and Gunnar Nygren. 2009. "Journalistic work: A profession under pressure?" *Journal of Media Business Studies* 6 (1): 37–59.

World Population Review. 2018. "2018 statistics for U.S. cities." Accessed June 15, 2018. http://worldpopulationreview.com/us-cities/.

Yaschur, Carolyn. 2012. "Shooting the shooter: How experience level affects photojournalistic coverage of a breaking news event." *Visual Communication Quarterly* 19 (3): 161–177.

Yu, Roger. 2014. "Battle of the brands: A newspaper war in New Orleans." *USA Today*, January 29, 2014. Accessed March 17, 2017. http://www.usatoday.com/story/money/business/2014/01/27/new-orleans-newspaper-war/4580561/.

Zelizer, Barbie. 2007. "On 'having been there': 'Eyewitnessing' as a journalistic key word." *Critical Studies in Media Communication* 24 (5): 408–428.

Index

Mary Lou Nemanic is an Associate Professor Emerita at the Pennsylvania State University. She is Co-founder/Co-director of Documentary America, the author of *One Day for Democracy: Independence Day and the Americanization of Iron Range Immigrants*, and co-editor of *Cultural Production in Virtual and Imagined Worlds*.